LEADING
THE Presence-Driven
CHURCH

JOHN PIIPPO

WESTBOW
PRESS®
A DIVISION OF THOMAS NELSON
& ZONDERVAN

WestBow Press books may be ordered through booksellers or by contacting:

WestBow Press
A Division of Thomas Nelson & Zondervan
1663 Liberty Drive
Bloomington, IN 47403
www.westbowpress.com
1 (866) 928-1240

ISBN: 978-1-9736-1091-5 (sc)
ISBN: 978-1-9736-1093-9 (hc)
ISBN: 978-1-9736-1092-2 (e)

Library of Congress Control Number: 2017919215

Print information available on the last page.

WestBow Press rev. date: 12/18/2017

DEDICATION

To my brothers and sisters at Redeemer Fellowship Church

CONTENTS

ACKNOWLEDGMENTS

My thanks to the many who have encouraged and supported my passion and desire to communicate the belief that God's Church can be consumed and accompanied by God's presence.

To Dave Nichols — your response to one of the first things I posted about this, and your ongoing support and input, have greatly encouraged me.

To Carol Dougherty-Steptoe — you have carried and developed my teachings further than I could have, and to places I would never have imagined.

To Don Follis — you have supported and helped me further the vision God has placed within me.

To Bob Myers — for your support and friendship and push back on my writings.

To Gloria Evans and my Sioux Falls friends — your prayers and affirmation have greatly encouraged me.

To my colleagues in Holy Spirit Renewal Ministries — thank you for your graciousness in giving me a platform to express my ideas, and for all Linda and I have learned from you about God's empowering presence.

To my precious sisters and brothers of our church, Redeemer Fellowship — your prayers and support and love for God's presence have provided the soil from which this book has grown.

To our home group — your loyal friendship and dialogue over the years have confirmed the ideas presented in this book.

To Lora Sue Hauser — your affirmation of the presence-driven church has meant much to me.

To my beautiful wife and life partner Linda — you are my living example of what it means to enter God's presence and respond in love and obedience.

1

INTRODUCTION

My life in Christ began with an experience.
An encounter.

And my world changed forever.

My salvation story began like this. I was twenty-one. I was a God-ignorer. I believed in God, but I paid no attention to him. In my day-to-day existence, God meant nothing to me. I was a practical atheist.[1]

I was a student at Northern Illinois University, living on campus in an apartment. One evening, my roommate informed me that he had met a campus minister. The campus minister wanted to come to our apartment and talk with us. My roommate said, "Sure."

Anticipating his arrival, I began thinking of questions he could not answer. I wanted to trap him and expose his stupidity.

The campus minister came. He didn't look like a minister to me. He was young, athletic, didn't have a beard, and wasn't wearing a collar and robe. We invited him to into our living room, and sat down to listen to him talk about religion.

---

[1] For all practical purposes, I lived as if God did not exist.

He told us about his experience with Jesus, and how his life had been changed by God. When he finished, I began hitting him with questions. He was gracious and polite in his answers. He did not seem agitated or worried by us. Finally, I asked the big question, hoping to confuse this freak of Jesus. I don't remember what the question was, only that I thought it up and could not wait to launch it towards his unprotected mind.

When the campus pastor heard The Question, he immediately responded, "I don't know the answer to that."

I had not anticipated this. My hope was he would try to make something up, or give some mindless statements that would expose his stupidity. Instead, he said what any honest person would have said. He was truthful. He didn't know. What a disappointment that was to me!

As I think back on this, I see how the tables had turned. Now, I was the vulnerable one. My flimsy fortress was crumbling. "But," he added, "I do believe there is a God, and that *this God loves you.*"

That's when it happened.

With those words, that old familiar cliché "God loves you," an inner revolution was kick-started. It got to me. It was inside me. It was palpable, visceral, existential. It was like a force, a movement. *I felt it.* I experienced it. I was churning inside. I could only think, "This is crazy! This is God, showing up in my apartment, and he loves me!"

Looking back, I see a chain of events preparing me for this. It wasn't something I planned, or programmed. That's how it happens with God. Not only do we *not* program God's activity in our lives, we *cannot* do this. The Holy Spirit is nonprogrammable and unpredictable. Underline this: <u>his ways are not our ways</u>.

God's presence, his nearness, his love, his transcendent whatever, walked past the fallen fortress walls of my heart and announced, "It's Me."

That's how *I* began. I soon learned I was in good existential company. This is how Saul became Paul. One day he is walking on a road in northern Israel. Then, Somebody touched him. There is nothing like a transcendent experience to change a life.

This is the thesis of my book. *Transcendent experiencing will change the life of a church.*

Such was my beginning with Jesus. It was not phenomenally the same as what happened to C.S. Lewis, but qualitatively similar. Lewis wrote:

> "As the dry bones shook and came together in that dreadful valley of Ezekiel's, so now a philosophical theorem, cerebrally entertained, began to stir and heave and throw off its grave cloths, and stood upright and became a living presence... He only said, "I am the Lord"; "I am that I am"; "I am." People who are naturally religious find difficulty in understanding the horror of such a revelation. Amiable agnostics will talk cheerfully about "man's search for God." To me, as I then was, they might as well have talked about the mouse's search for the cat."[2]

God found Paul and C.S. Lewis, and God found me. I was receptive. I was ready to hear that he existed, and that he loved me. I was ready to know him.

I know many pastors. Most of these women and men, my colleagues, began as I did, by an encounter with God's presence. I have heard their beautiful, amazing stories. I am inspired by them. I am more inspired by their tales of encountering God than I am by their theologies. I am uninterested in their theologies if they have not come out of experiences.

I have never gotten over my first encounter with Love. It was a purging baptism into an alternative kingdom. It was accompanied by an experiential knowing that refused to be reduced to logical syllogisms. People like C.S.

---

[2] C.S. Lewis, *Surprised by Joy* (New York: HarperCollins, 1955) p. 225.

Lewis were brought in kicking and screaming. Paul was struck blind. Others entered crying. I entered amazed. I stood amazed, in God's presence.

This is a book about the primacy, the centrality, of God and his unsurpassable presence. And what this means for the Church.[3] The presence of God is the core, the *sine qua non*, of mere Christianity. God's presence is what will win the day over the present powers of darkness. I will show what it means for a church to be presence-driven, and what leadership looks like in a presence-driven church.

My concern is that our secular, post-Jesus culture has squeezed this out of the souls of God's followers. I have listened to many pastors and leaders over the decades, and conclude that the American Church will steal our experiential knowledge of God if we allow it.[4]

I remember a pastor named Joe. He was in a class on prayer that I taught at Northern Baptist Theological Seminary. On the first day of class, Joe returned from the assigned hour of solitary praying. He was crying. He confessed, before the class, "I haven't done that in twenty years. And, I heard God tell me that he loved me." On that day, Joe came home.

Love is an unscripted encounter that cannot be captured in the steel nets of literal language. Love is an experience, not a theory. God *is* love. Every experience of God is a love-encounter. This is how many of us began. This is how I began. The consumer-driven church will rob us of this.[5]

This book is a call for pastors and Christian leaders to return home, which is the presence of God. It is a call to dwell in the House of God, rather than

---

[3] Throughout I will capitalize "Church" to mean either the Church universal or, more specifically, the American Church (the Western Church).
[4] By "American Church" I mean Church that has accommodated itself to American/Western culture, rather than maintaining its distinctives.
[5] By "Consumer-Driven Church," I mean Church that focuses on giving people what they are shopping for, rather than on what their souls are desperate for.

the House of Fear.[6] It is a call to cultivate this, by abiding in God's presence. It is a summons to lead others into the living waters and pure atmosphere of God's presence. It is a mandate to be leaders in God's Presence-Driven Church.

LEADERSHIP STEPS AND SUGGESTIONS

At the end of every chapter I will share ideas that relate to leadership in a presence-driven church. Most of these come out of my own experience. They may not be relevant to your church.

That is the nature of the presence-driven church; viz., that God will lead us uniquely, carving out his grace according to our personal, corporate, and cultural situatedness. But there is one enduring constant, and it is God, presencing himself among us. I will argue that, without this, it's not really Church.

So, here are a few suggestions, as we begin.

I am guessing that, when you became a follower of Jesus, it was due more to experience than to theory. What was your experience like?

God found you, in an encounter. Remember this. Share it with your people.

Have some of your people share their testimonies of how they began their life in Christ. How did God rescue them? Pay attention to, draw attention to, the experiential qualities of their stories.

Thank God, privately and publicly, for how he has revealed himself experientially to you, and to others.

---

[6] See Henri Nouwen, *Lifesigns: Intimacy, Fecundity, and Ecstasy in Christian Perspective* (New York: Image Books, 1986).

2

THE CASE FOR EXPERIENCE

When I was a teen, my father took me to watch fast cars race a quarter mile at the Rockford Dragway.[1] The steward of the dragway was a friend of dad. We were given pit passes to see the cars and drivers up close.

That night was special. A drag racer named Art Arfons was there, with his famous "Green Monster." This vehicle was a jet engine fastened to the frame of a car. As we entered the pit we were handed ear plugs. The Green Monster held the world land speed record of 576 mph. It went from 0-60 in three seconds. It was loud! At the time, my mode of transportation was a red Nash Rambler. It accelerated from 0-60 in three minutes. It, too, was loud, but for different reasons.

That was an exciting night! It was made even better when dad's friend showed me his car. It was a 1963 Ford Shelby Cobra. Just the name "Cobra" exudes danger, in a way "Rambler" does not. I have an image of my Rambler sauntering, strolling, and meandering down the quarter mile strip on its way to a picnic.

The Cobra went 0-60 in five seconds. Dad's friend looked at me and asked, "Would you like to ride with me to open up the evening?" Yes (power!). And no (danger!).

---

[1] Rockford, Illinois.

I said yes.

I sat in the passenger's seat, and went for the fastest quarter mile I had ever experienced. What teenaged boy didn't like fast cars? That night I grew in knowledge of power and speed. I had seen magazines and television shows on drag racing. I loved looking at cool cars. But all the reading in the world did not compare with experiencing the Shelby Cobra for myself.

In this book I am arguing that churches must be presence-driven, because *experience gives knowledge that theory cannot*. Better is one quarter mile raced, than a thousand automotive theories read.

It is the same with God.

Therefore, presence-driven churches value experience. Experience, not theory, breeds conviction. We want our people to *know* Christ, not just know *about* him. The biblical Greek word *gnosis* means *understanding by experience*. Better is one day experiencing God, than a thousand sermons about God.

One thing about an experience is this: it cannot be fully captured in words. When my son Josh graduated from high school, my present to him was a trip to the Grand Canyon. We flew into Phoenix, where I picked up a rental car. It was an orange Mustang. What a beautiful beginning! We drove the Mustang north to our hotel in Williams, Arizona. The next day we cruised to immerse ourselves in the canyon.

Seeing the Grand Canyon with our own eyes was better than reading about it. Photos are awesome, but wither before the real thing. I could have camped out on the rim and spent days beholding it. To walk into the canyon, descending on its trails, is a nondiscursive experience.[2]

Words can gesture towards the experience, but in the end you have to be there yourself. Actually, this is true of any experience, even mundane ones. I now see my coffee cup. I hold it in my hand. I lift it to my mouth. I taste the

---

[2] By "nondiscursive experience" I mean: one cannot adequately discourse about it.

java. I feel it slip-sliding down my throat. I sense the effects of the caffeine. How shall I describe this, in words? The experience of the coffee and the cup is epistemically superior to any poem I might write, or any essay I might pen, about the coffee encounter. In the end, if you really want to know, you must see my cup, hold it, and taste for yourself that the coffee is good.

Religious experience is the same. To know God, we must experience God.

We fall short of understanding the stories in the Bible if we lack the kind of experiences those stories describe.[3] "Religion," writes Wayne Proudfoot, "has always been an experiential matter. It is not just a set of creedal statements or a collection of rites."[4]

The entire Bible is about knowing God by experience. God promises experiential knowledge to those who abide in Jesus, and follow.

Jesus told his disciples that, even though he was going to die on a cross, he would be with them, always. I assume the words "with you" are about some kind of actual experience. If God is not with me, experientially, then what good is he to me?

What I deeply need is God, not words about God. I need God to walk before, with, and behind me in this desacralized, disenchanted world. If this is not real, experientially, then at most I am left with deism, and at worst I am an atheist.[5]

I need God with me presently, because I am not smart enough to guide my own life, much less assist others on the way. I am not powerful enough to

---

[3] This is at the core of Craig Keener's thesis in his book *Spirit Hermeneutics: Reading Scripture in Light of Pentecost,* (Grand Rapids: Eerdmans, 2017).

[4] Wayne Proudfoot, *Religious Experience* (Berkeley and Los Angeles: University of California Press, 1985), p. xi.

[5] See Clark Pinnock's introduction to Charles Kraft, *Christianity with Power: Your Worldview and Experience of the Supernatural* (Eugene, Oregon: Wipf and Stock, 1989). When God is not known by experiential love and power, we have "practical atheism." For all practical purposes, God does not exist.

halt the eroding wasting-away of my physical body, much less heal others. I am not loving enough to overwhelm my enemies, and even struggle with loving myself. I am a flower that emerges from the ground, blooms, then quickly withers and dies. I am an ocean wave that crashes and recedes. I am weak in time and space, body and mind, strength and soul, a virtually unknown speck of matter in an ever-cycling faceless mass of humanity, situated in a universe that is beyond all human comprehension.

That's me. That's us. We are fragile, and small.

I am weak, but God is strong. This is my condition. I need help. On my own I am not strong enough, knowledgeable enough, or loving enough to do the job God asks of me. God, however, is omnibenevolent, omnipotent, and omniscient.[6] If I could connect with God, the resources that are his being could flow into me. I need *God with me*.

Is not this what we are promised? The virgin will conceive and give birth to a son, and they will call him *Immanuel* (which means *"God with us"*).[7] I assume this does not mean God is with me, in theory.

Real, biblical Christianity is not formulaic ritualistic behavior. Nor is it mind-numbing,[8] entertainment-induced "happiness." In Christ, the ancient promise takes on human skin and bone. God comes near, to us. If this is not true, then the command to love God with all our being would be like loving a statement, or kissing an abstract entity like the number seven, or hugging a Platonic form.

This is why I am still a Christian.

I follow Jesus today, because I know, and have been known by him. I have been met by Jesus. I talk with him throughout the day. My spiritual palate

---

[6] God has more essential attributes than this. On the attributes of God there is no better resource than Wayne Grudem's *Systematic Theology* (Grand Rapids: Zondervan, 1994), chapters 11-14.

[7] Matthew 1:23.

[8] Passive.

savors his redemptive goodness. My eyes see his power and glory. I have a bookshelf of journal entries, cataloguing the adventures of Immanuel and me.

James McDonald writes:

> "A real encounter with the living God changes everything. First, it magnifies the Lord, and then it puts me and my ego and my sin and my burdens all in their rightful place.
>
> That is what church is supposed to do and be. Not an encounter with the glory of God in creation but an encounter with God in a different, even more awesome way that only church can provide. However, church today as a weekly experience with the manifest glory of God is the greatest lack we face. The lost are not found because God's glory is not revealed in church. Children wander because church is pathetically predictable or shamefully entertaining but hardly ever authentically God."[9]

Experiencing God changes me. In this chapter I am making the case for knowing God by experience, as central to the biblical narrative, and to what Church is supposed to be.

EXPERIENTIAL KNOWING

"When I entered your church's sanctuary, I felt the presence of God."

"Often, when I enter your sanctuary on a Sunday morning, I begin to cry."

"Surely the Lord is in this sanctuary."

---

[9] James McDonald, *Vertical Church: What Every Heart Longs For. What Every Church Can Be* (Colorado Springs: David C. Cook, 2012), Kindle Locations 56-61

Over my twenty-five years at Redeemer, I have heard these words many times, in a variety of permutations, spoken by people new to our Jesus-community.

"I sensed God's peace as I approached your building."

"I encountered God's power as I worshiped with your people."

I experience this, too. This is how Church should be. As Jesus-followers we stand in fields of God's power and grace.[10] Our new status is existence within the Trinitarian being of God.[11] We encounter, regularly, the earth-shattering presence of God. We say, "Surely the Lord is in *this place*."[12]

This is Real Church; viz., a people who host the presence of God. We are portable temples, individually[13] and corporately.[14] God comes to dwell among his people, inhabiting his lovers in their singular hearts and their plural communities. The habitation of God is a visceral, experiential reality, not just a propositional truth. One *feels* God, within and without. As God lavishly pours his love into our hearts, this is, precisely and Hebraically, best understood as a feeling.[15]

Part of my evangelical heritage is to pause at this point, and warn me about the dangers of "feelings." Reason, I was told, is the engine of the train, and feelings are the caboose. Feelings are not in our control, and it is not a good thing to be out of control.

---

[10] "Since we have been justified through faith, we have peace with God through our Lord Jesus Christ, ² through whom we have gained access by faith into this grace in which we now stand." Romans 5:1-2

[11] See Dallas Willard, *Living in Christ's Presence: Final Words on Heaven and the Kingdom of God* (Downers Grove: InterVarsity, 2017). This is the reality Jesus shares with his disciples in John chapters fourteen and fifteen. For the ministerial implications of this, see Stephen Seamands, *Ministry in the Image of God: The Trinitarian Shape of Christian Service* (Downers Grove: InterVarsity, 2006).

[12] Genesis 28:16.

[13] I Corinthians 3:16. The word 'you' is singular.

[14] I Corinthians 6:19. The word 'you' is plural.

[15] I say "Hebraically," meaning ancient and contemporary Jewish culture is anti-Cartesian; viz., persons are not emotionally detached "thinking things."

As a long time professor of logic, and even longer as a Finnish male, I understand this. My response is to point out the other side; viz., the dangers and vacuities of theories and intellectual reasoning without feelings. All talk about God's "love" is meaning-deficient if it does not include feeling. What a tragedy it would be to say to Linda, "I love you, but have no feeling for you." The core of my faith in Jesus is loving him, with much feeling, and being loved by him, which elicits feelings.[16]

When I was twenty-four, about to marry Linda, our campus pastor, John Peterson, recommended I read Walter Trobisch's *Love Is a Feeling to Be Learned*. I suspect John knew I had much to learn about feelings. Love is a feeling, as well as an action. Consider these words from Robert Barclay, written in 1701.

> "When I came into the silent assemblies of God's people,
> I felt a secret power among them, which touched my heart.
> And as I gave way to it, I found the evil in me weakening,
> and the good lifted up. Thus it was that I was knit into
> them and united with them. And I hungered more and
> more for the increase of this power and life until I could
> feel myself perfectly redeemed."[17]

Thank God that he allows us to experience him! Thank God he made us to feel as well as to think!

It is important to remember that the target of Jesus' mission was the rescue and renovation of the human heart.[18] This salvation is comprehensive, and includes our emotions, feelings, bodies, and minds. Emotions and feelings, both describable and indescribable, are included in our heart. Such

---

[16] I do think intellectual reasoning has a place in the Christian life. I recently retired from seventeen years of teaching logic at our local county community college.

[17] In Richard Foster, *Sanctuary of the Soul: Journey Into Meditative Prayer* (Downers Grove: InterVarsity, 2011), Kindle Locations 302-304.

[18] See, e.g., Dallas Willard, *Renovation of the Heart* (Carol Stream, Illinois: NavPress, 2012).

things are experienced, rather than reasoned out as conclusions of a logical argument.[19]

In the presence-driven church people are allowed to have and share experiences-with-feelings that transcend human reason. This is important, since "many committed Christians believe in God not primarily because of *argument* but because of *experience* — they have an intuitive sense of God's presence."[20]

It is hard, and ultimately impossible, to explain authentic religious experience in literal language. Presence-driven followers of Jesus have God-encounters that cannot be captured in literal language. One cannot speak of them without remainder. They transcend discourse. They are ways of knowing something, like my new knowledge of the Grand Canyon upon experiencing it. The presence-driven church allows for such experiences of God, and expects them to happen.

It is important to understand that our language has limits. The being of God cannot be fully captured by our words. Perhaps this is one reason the apostle Paul cautions us that the kingdom of God is not a matter of talk, but of power.[21] When it comes to limit-experiences, too much talking leads to misunderstanding.

A non-discursive experience is an experience that is felt and "known" as real, but which cannot be captured in literal explanations.[22] One has such experiences, but cannot exhaustively discourse about them.[23] This is when

---

[19] Our feelings cannot be argued with or argued for. Feelings are not chosen. They are, as Alvin Plantinga might say, "properly basic."

[20] Michael Rota, *Taking Pascal's Wager: Faith, Evidence and the Abundant Life* (Downers Grove: Intervarsity, 2016), Kindle Location 140.

[21] I Corinthians 4:20.

[22] Nearly all language was originally metaphorical. Even the word 'is' is from the Sanskrit *asmi*, which means "to breathe."

[23] One very good book about "knowing that you know that you know" is James K. A. Smith, *Thinking in Tongues: Pentecostal Contributions to Christian Philosophy* (Grand Rapids: Eerdmans, 2010).

experiencers resort to art, poetry, music, or fiction, as ways of pointing towards the essentially beyond-us and indescribable.

I have experienced God in a variety of ways, all of which are ultimately non-discursive.[24] I have transcendent God-encounters every week, usually every day. This is how it should be, right, if God is truly with me? I have experiences with Linda every day. We live in the same home, so this makes sense. Scripture tells me that God has made his home in me.[25] Therefore, unless God is staying isolated in his room, I talk with him, encounter him, and experience him daily. Like the old hymn states, "He walks with me, and He talks with me, and He tells me I am His own." All the time.

These experiences are hard to describe. To understand this, you have to meet up with him yourself. When God encounters me, it is often hard to say anything coherent. This is because none of us has epistemic access to the being of God.[26] We have no clue about what it's really like to be all-knowing, all-loving, and all-powerful. Famously, as Thomas Nagel has told us, we don't even know what it is like to be a bat.[27]

German theologian Karl Barth said God was so "wholly other" that we cannot even talk about God existing, "because to say he exists is to suggest that his reality shares something of the reality of everything else that exists. But God's being is so radically different from ours that the word "exists" cannot do justice to his existence. Thus we cannot say that God "exists.""[28]

---

[24] Every experience has a non-discursive quality. Some are more non-discursive than others.

[25] John 14:23.

[26] This is the core belief of "skeptical theism." Skeptical theism is not skeptical of the existence of God. It is skeptical of our human ability to understand God and his ways. Examples of skeptical theists include Alvin Plantinga, Peter van Inwagen, and Steven Wykstra.

[27] Philosopher Thomas Nagel, in his famous essay "What Is It Like to Be a Bat?", concludes we could never, in principle, know the answer. If we could never know what it is like to be a bat, how much less could we know what it is like to be God?

[28] Mark Galli, "Our Relation to God Is Ungodly," Christianity Today, October 2017, Vol. 61, No. 8, p. 6.

Who can come close to capturing the reality of our God who infinitely transcends our puny cognitive capacities?

In this chapter I am making a case for experience as a form of knowing that is in some ways superior to logical reasoning and theorizing. The pastoral implication is this: I must allow my people to experience God in ways that are biblical, yet unfamiliar to my intellectual capacities. No human cognitive box can contain the fullness of the Lord. With this, the caboose of feelings has become an engine of knowledge that drives us.

In a presence-driven church it is important to spotlight peoples' experiences with God. Make a place for them to share their God-encounters. Invite them to share their stories. As much as I love logic and theorizing, I have rarely been overwhelmed by logical rules of inference such as *modus ponens*.[29] But stories of my peoples' experiences with God fill me with joy, move me to tears, and create hope and expectation.

The expression of non-discursive experiences is confessional and testimonial. There is a sense in which these stories cannot be refuted. What does that mean? Say, for example, that I now feel "joy." I make the statement, "Now I feel joyful." It would be odd for someone to respond, "You're wrong."

In a presence-driven church people have experiences of God. Many in my church have dreams and visions, through which God speaks to them. Some see angels,[30] in the sanctuary, on Sunday mornings! There might be times I wonder about the veridicality of these angel-sightings, but I usually don't question the people about them. I believe most of them, because I have been with these people for twenty-five years as their pastor. I trust them. I know

---

[29] *Modus ponens* is a classic logical syllogism that goes like this: 1) If p, then q. 2) p. 3) Therefore, q. On a few occasions, I have rejoiced over this.

[30] See, e.g., Jack Hayford, *Glory On Your House* (Grand Rapids: Chosen Books, 1982).

of their devotion to Jesus.[31] This relates, I think, to Oxford philosopher Richard Swinburne's "principle of credulity."[32] My people are credible witnesses.

It is difficult to evaluate another person's experience. Imagine I say to you, "I felt God close to me today." Even a philosophical materialist could not doubt that, today, I had some kind of numinous experience, which I describe as God being with me. Some might doubt that the cause of my experience was "God." I understand that. But their doubt has no effect on my experience, and my interpretation of it. Their doubt does not make *me* a doubter.

I see no reason to disbelieve my experiences because others do not have them. A presence-driven pastor must understand this, because in the presence-driven church your people will have experiences with God, often unlike any you have had.

Knowing by experience is persuasive. Individual and corporate experiences with God are powerful convincers. Presence-driven people are more persuaded by experiences than they are persuaded by words. To them, this is the kingdom of God, not as a matter of discourse, but of transcendent power.

Analytic philosopher William P. Alston calls this "theistic experience." He writes:

---

[31] I have had many seminary students share similar experiences with me. One example is a pastor from Pakistan. I sent my class out of the room to find a place to pray for an hour. When he returned from praying he shared that he was kneeling, when he felt a tap on his shoulder. He looked up, and there stood a person dressed in white. This person said, "I am with you. You are going to be OK." He had never had that happen before. It gave him great confidence, which he needed, since he and other pastors were experiencing persecution in Pakistan.

[32] In Richard Swinburne, *The Existence of God* (Oxford: Clarendon, 1979), chapter 13. If it seems (epistemically) to a subject S that x is present, then probably x is present.'

I "mean it to range over all experiences that are taken by the experiencer to be an awareness of God (where God is thought of theistically). I impose no restrictions on its phenomenal quality. It could be a rapturous loss of conscious self-identity in the mystical unity with God; it could involve "visions and voices"; it could be an awareness of God through the experience of nature, the words of the Bible, or the interaction with other persons; it could be a background sense of the presence of God, sustaining one in one's ongoing activities. Thus, the category is demarcated by what cognitive significance the subject takes it to have, rather than by any distinctive phenomenal feel."[33]

If the noetic framework (worldview) of Christian theism is true, then we can *expect* to experience God. God has made us in his image, has placed a moral consciousness within us, has revealed himself in the creation, and desires for us to know him. Within this worldview, one normally expects experiential encounters with God. They come to us, as Alston says, like sense-experiences. They come to me on Monday morning, as I am alone in prayer. They come to me in the small group Linda and I are part of. They happen on Sunday mornings, every one of them.

These non-discursive encounters with God cannot be captured in the steel nets of literal language. This is because "experience" *qua* experience has what French philosopher Paul Ricoeur called a "surplus of meaning." "Words" never capture all of experience, or reality. Never. All experiencing has a non-discursive quality.[34] Be careful, pastors, that you do not attempt to reduce the transcendent experiences of your people to your verbal limitations.

---

[33] Ib.

[34] Here the relationship, if any, of words to experiencing leads to volumes of discussion in areas such as linguistic semantics and philosophy of language.

I am defending experience by pointing to the limitations of descriptive language.[35] Even a sentence as seemingly simple as "I see a tree" is, phenomenally, incomplete. Consider the experience of sitting on an ocean beach, watching the sunset with the person you are falling in love with. Ricoeur calls such experiences "limit-experiences"; viz., experiences that arise outside the limits of thought and language. But people want to express, in words, these events. For that, Ricoeur says, a "limit-language" is needed, such as metaphorical expression. So-called "literal language" cannot express limit-experiences.[36]

Presence-driven Jesus-followers have limit-experiences that move into the arena of non-discursiveness. A presence-driven pastor will not be threatened by this. Indeed, they will be nourished and encouraged by such experiences.

At Redeemer, we allow for testimonies of God's presence in our Sunday morning worship events. I have my own stories of being encountered by God. Among God-experiences I consistently have are:

- A sense that God is with me
- Numinous experiences of awe and wonder (not mere "Einsteinian wonder"[37])
- God speaking to me
- God leading me
- God comforting me
- God's love expressed towards me
- God's Spirit convicting me
- God directing me

[35] See Charles Taylor, *The Language Animal* (Cambridge: Belknap, 2016). Taylor makes a distinction between language as "designative/instrumental," and language as "constitutive/expressive." Most Westerners are locked into the former.
[36] See Paul Ricoeur, *The Rule of Metaphor: The Creation of Meaning in Language* (Toronto: University of Toronto, 1975), and *Interpretation Theory: Discourse and the Surplus of Meaning* (Fort Worth: Texas Christian University Press, 1976). In my doctoral dissertation on metaphor theory I wrote extensively on understanding the concept of "literal."
[37] "Einsteinian wonder" refers to 1) being awed by nature; and 2) reducing transcendent causes to purely natural causes.

- Overwhelming experience of God
- God revealing more of himself to me

These experiences are often mediated through:

- Corporate worship
- Individuals
- Solitary times of prayer
- Study of the Christian scriptures
- Observing the creation
- In difficult and testing situations

Sometimes I experience God in an unmediated way. How do I recognize this? I discern such things to be experiences of God because:

- I spend many hours a week praying (for the past 40+ years).
- I saturate myself in the Christian scriptures.
- I have studied the history of Christian spirituality.
- I keep a spiritual journal and, over the past 3 years, have 3500+ pages of journal entries having to do with God experiences, and the voice of God to spoken to me.
- I hang out with people who do all of the above.
- I've taught this experience in various seminaries, conferences, in the United States and around the world. I've taught this material to over four thousand pastors and leaders. I have gained, to a degree, a multi-ethnic perspective on the subject of experiencing God.

Knowledge by experience is not secondary, inferior knowledge. Neither is it *not* a way of knowing at all. It is common, needed, available, and in ways superior to theories and information.

Linda and I recently met up with our son Dan and his wife Allie in Chicago. We took the Chicago Architectural Boat Tour, a ninety-minute cruise up the Chicago River. The towering buildings of Chicago flanked us on both sides. My neck ached from looking up, as I took over 200 photos.

The photos, for me, spoke louder than words. The experience spoke louder than the photos. When people asked, "How was the cruise?", I pulled up the photos and showed them. Then I added, "You really have to take the tour for yourself."

In this chapter I have made a case for the primacy of experience when it comes to knowing God. You have to taste God for yourself. Then, you will know. This is important for presence-driven leaders to understand, since God's presence is known in feelings, emotions, and mediated through our five senses. The reality of experiencing God is foundational in a presence-driven church.

LEADERSHIP STEPS AND SUGGESTIONS

Pastors and leaders must spend much time in God's presence. Make this your first priority. Share with your people when, and how, you are doing this.

Keep a spiritual journal, which is a record of the voice and activity of God in your life.

Share your experiences of God with your church family.

If you have a church staff, use your meetings to share stories of how you are experiencing God. Ask each other questions, like, "What has God been doing in your life?" "What has God been saying to you?"

Make places for your people to share testimonies of God's activity in their lives.

In preaching and teaching, emphasize the value and place of the Hebraic nature of "knowing" as experiencing. Preach about some of the numerous God-encounters in the Scriptures.

Cultivate an atmosphere of expectation.

3

THE "PRESENCE MOTIF"

Last summer I experienced a moment of culinary terror. Linda and I went to P.F. Chang's in Ann Arbor. We like this restaurant. No matter what happened to us that night, we will go again.

I ordered the entrée I mostly get when I'm at P.F. Chang's. The waiter left, and Linda and I spent time talking as we awaited the coming of the cuisine. It seemed to take longer than usual. Eventually, the waiter returned, to utter words I will never forget: "I am sorry, sir. We are out of rice."

And there was silence in the heavens.

I was stunned. I thought of logical impossibilities, like square circles, married bachelors, and Cartesian mountains without valleys. An Asian restaurant with no rice? Logically impossible!

I saw the manager walking from table to table, confessing ricelessness to the patrons. When he got to us I had to ask, "How could this be so?" He replied, "They are having trouble in the kitchen."

"They?" My thought was, "You had better get in that kitchen and fix this barren situation!"

Our experience at P.F. Chang's brought back a memory of a similar event. It was a sunny morning in the 1980s. Linda and I lived in East Lansing,

Michigan. That day we went to breakfast at International House of Pancakes. I ordered pancakes.

There was no maple syrup on the table.

When it comes to pancakes, I am a purist. I don't want the strawberry syrup or the blueberry syrup or the fruity bacon syrup. So, desiring maple syrup, I asked:

"May I have some maple syrup please?"

"Sorry," said the waitress. "We're out of maple syrup."

My response was: nothingness.

These two experiences were painful, but cannot be compared to The Big Absence two summers ago.

Linda and I were driving from Monroe to Chicago. We were on the Indiana Tollway, and stopped at a rest area for lunch. Linda went to one of the fast food places and got a salad. I got in line at Kentucky Fried Chicken.

I can see the scene, as if it were happening now. Three of us were in line. There was a man in front of me at the counter. I was behind him, with a third man behind me. Three of us, about to be disenchanted.

Often, in life, we view events through the framework of what we are currently immersed in. At Redeemer, I was in the thick of preaching through the book of *Revelation*. I was thinking about *Revelation* all the time! I was reading and re-reading the text, looking at it in the Greek language, and studying the best commentaries on the subject. *Revelation* was my constant meditation.

The Greek title is *The Apocalypse*. *Apocalypto* means "an uncovering," an "unveiling." Like someone who lifts the lid on a simmering pot of stew to see and smell the ingredients, in *The Apocalypse* God lifts the lid of what is to happen cosmically, and John the Apostle is allowed to look inside. That day, at KFC, the lid was about to be lifted, and I would look inside.

"I want a three-piece chicken dinner," said the first man.

"I am sorry, sir," said the hostess at the KFC on the Indiana Tollway in the summer of 2015, "but we are out of chicken."

With those words the lid blew off. A fiery abyss appeared to my right. I heard the hoofbeats of Four Horsemen thundering in the distance. I saw bowls poured out upon the earth. I heard the cries of saints beneath the Great White Throne. The man in front of me said nothing. He just walked away, like a floating, drifting planet that lost its sun, or perhaps its faith.

I felt a tap on my shoulder, and a voice spoke to me. I did not turn around as the man behind me said, "Did you hear what I heard?" Speechless, I nodded my head up and down. I left the little three-man queue and walked to where Linda was sitting. "No way!" she said, in unbelief.

My expectation, when going to Kentucky Fried Chicken, is to be served chicken. When I am at a pancake house, I expect maple syrup. When I am at an Asian restaurant, I expect rice. Anything less is unacceptable and irrational. It is the same with God's presence. When I am with the Church, I expect to encounter God. Real Church is a Temple. Temples house the presence of God. Anything less than God in the Temple is unacceptable.

I am like Moses, who despaired at the thought of God withdrawing his presence from the people. Moses pleaded, saying, "God, if your presence does not go with us, we are not going!"[1]

"Do not," appealed the psalmist, "cast me away from your presence." The ultimate suffering and punishment is separation from the presence of God.

---

[1] Exodus 33:15-16.

I see a world desperate for the presence of God. They long and pant, like thirsty deer in the Judean wilderness, for an experiential encounter with God. Anything less is unsatisfactory.

I pastor a presence-driven church, not a program-driven or purpose-driven church.[2] We are a church for anyone who thirsts for God. I am taken by the possibility that the people of God can be guided and led by the Spirit of God. If this is true, then the primary thing a pastor must do is connect with God. As a pastor, I must resolutely abide in the presence of Christ.[3] I don't want to move without God with me.

I must shepherd my people into the presence of God. Jesus-following pastors and leaders guide their people into an abiding relationship with Christ. It is precisely in this mutual, indwelling intimacy, that the Spirit leads, loves, empowers, and heals.

My church community is an experiment in being led by God. One result is that my people recognize the One doing the leading and producing the fruitfulness is not some mere human leader, but the brilliance of God himself. A true leader's greatness lies in their not-so-greatness, and their trust in God's infinite capacities.[4]

In this chapter I am making the case for Emmanuel, God with us. If this isn't the Church's primal reality, the sun around which everything orbits, then we're just leading our own selves. I've been there, done that, and, like Moses, don't want to go there again.

---

[2] Presence precedes programming and purpose. I appreciated and gained from Rick Warren's writings on the Purpose-Driven Church. I feel he would agree with the priority of presence over purpose. I would change "purpose" to concepts such as "calling" and "obedience."

[3] See John chapters fourteen and fifteen.

[4] This corporate realization will ignite worship as a Movement.

THE PRESENCE OF GOD IS
THE CHURCH'S GREAT DISTINCTIVE

The Church's great distinctive is this: We have God, and God's presence. We have answers to the ultimate questions. We have Christ in us, the hope of glory. That's not bad. And, this core distinctive costs no money to maintain. God doesn't have a fee for his appearing.

Can a church have culturally relevant things? I believe so. But these things, as awesome as they might be, are not manifestations of our great distinctive. The Gospel is relevant, but a presence-driven church is not striving to be relevant. Os Guinness writes:

> "Rarely has the church seen so many of its leaders solemnly presenting the faith in public in so many weak, trite, foolish, disastrous, and even disloyal ways as today...
>
> This monumental and destructive carelessness has coincided exactly with a mania for relevance and reinvention that has gripped the church. So a disconcerting question arises: *How on earth have we Christians become so irrelevant when we have tried so hard to be relevant?* And by what law or logic is it possible to steer determinedly in one direction but end up in completely the opposite direction?... We are confronted by an embarrassing fact: Never have Christians pursued relevance more strenuously; never have Christians been more irrelevant."[5]

It's not evil for a church to have a fair-trade coffee bar. I probably like coffee more than you do. Coffee-drinking was so much a part of my Finnish heritage that my grandmother literally had tears in her eyes when she learned I started to drink it. To her, I finally joined the Finnish Faith Community. But something has gone wrong when God communicates to us one thing

---

[5] Os Guinness, *Prophetic Untimeliness: A Challenge to the Idol of Relevance* (Grand Rapids: Baker, 2003), p. II.

("better is one day in my presence"), and it gets transcripted as another thing ("better is one day with my barista").

In the First Testament, the greatest thing for a person to know is God's presence. To experience God is to know God. Hebrew "knowing" (*yadah*) is essentially experiential.[6] This greatest thing is what makes Church stand out.

Moses, In Exodus 33:15-16, appeals to God this way:

> And he said to him, "If your <u>presence</u> will not go with me, do not bring us up from here. [16] For how shall it be known that I have found favor in your sight, I and your people? Is it not in your going with us, so that we are <u>distinct</u>, I and your people, from every other people on the face of the earth?"

The appeal of Moses is an example of what Gordon Fee has called "the presence motif."[7] The presence motif carves a deep river that runs throughout Scripture. The reason "better is one day in your courts than a thousand elsewhere" is because God's desired, radiant, earth-shattering presence is there. Isaiah woefully wilts when encountered by the presence of God in the Temple.[8] In the gospels, the reason the Temple will no longer stand is because the religious leaders "shut the door to the kingdom of heaven."[9] God's reigning presence is gone!

The presence motif extends to the biblical meaning of the word "spiritual." To be "spiritual" *is* to be in God's presence. Fee, in his commentary on First Corinthians, argues that the basic issue in the Corinthian church, for Paul, is about the meaning of *pneumatikos*; that is, the meaning of "spiritual." What

---

[6] The Hebrew concept of "knowledge" is seen, e.g., in Genesis, where Abram "knew" Sarah. Such knowledge is personal, and experiential. On this kind of knowing see Michael Polanyi, *Personal Knowledge: Towards a Post-Critical Philosophy* (Chicago: University of Chicago, 1958).

[7] See especially Gordon Fee, *God's Empowering Presence* (Grand Rapids: Baker, 2009).

[8] Isaiah 6.

[9] See Matthew 23:13.

is it to be a "spiritual" person? Fee believes "their understanding of being *pneumatikos* is most likely related to their experience of Spirit inspiration."[10] From Paul's point of view, when someone says, "She is a spiritual person," it means, "She experiences the presence of God."

Christian spirituality concerns, primordially, *experience.* A person's spirit experiences the presence of the Spirit of God. To be "spiritual" is to be in God's presence; to be "unspiritual" is to be apart from God's presence. This is the presence motif, applied to personhood.

In this chapter I am claiming God's *experienced presence* is the central theme of Scripture. The beating heart of the Bible is the presence of God. It really *is* all about God, from Genesis to Revelation, and in between. Here are some more examples.

We see the presence motif in Psalm 46:10, which reads, "Be still, and know that I am God." To "be still" means, literally, to "cease struggling." We must stop resisting God's presence, and surrender to God. Our spirit is something that can either surrender or resist. When surrendered to God as he presences with us, we are, in the best sense, "spiritual." To be wholly surrendered to God is a way of being in the presence of God. One cannot be in God's presence unless they have surrendered to him. Therefore, *be still, and experience God.*

Hebrews 6:19 says, "We have this hope as an anchor for the soul, firm and secure." To be in God's presence means to cease from certain activities so our spirit, like a ship, might be anchored to God, who is the dock. To be spiritual is to live securely anchored to God's Holy Spirit. Conversely, our spirit is lost when it is restless, and drifts from God's presence. With this metaphor we see that our spirit is something that can be either securely anchored, or drift. To be anchored to God is a way of being in God's presence. *We experience the safety of God's presence when we are anchored to him.*

---

[10] Gordon Fee, *The First Epistle to the Corinthians* (Grand Rapids: Eerdmans, 2014), p. 10

Psalm 86:11 reads, "Give me an undivided heart, that I may fear your name." The human heart can either be divided or whole. The implication is that we cannot both be in God's presence and simultaneously attend to someone or something else. One cannot multi-task the God-relationship. *An undivided heart is required to experience God's presence.*

Henri Nouwen has said that the basic question of the spiritual life is: Who do you belong to? To live out of God's presence is to be, as James 1:8 says, *dipsuchos*. It is to have "two psyches," to be "two-hearted." In such a condition the spirit is divided regarding its allegiance. In a state of spiritual *dipsuchos* the human spirit has two lovers. I have found it often happens that when I go alone to a quiet place to pray, I am shown how conflicted my spirit may be. Therefore, spirit is something that can be either whole or fragmented. *Only the whole-hearted are blessed, for they shall experience the presence of God.*

I am making a case for the pervasiveness of the presence motif in Scripture. Another biblical presence-metaphor is a cathartic (cleansing) metaphor: "Create in me a clean heart, O God."[11] And, "Cleanse me with hyssop, and I shall be clean; wash me and I shall be whiter than snow."[12] Purity of heart is required to dwell in God's presence. Jesus tells us that only the pure in heart shall experience (see/know) the presence of God.[13] *Blessed are the mono-taskers, for they shall experience God.*

To have a pure heart, as the Danish philosopher Soren Kierkegaard wrote, is "to will one thing."[14] Conversely, our hearts can be "stained," "blemished," covered with "blots," and thus "impure." Sin creates a barrier to God's presence. The central biblical image of sin is "stain." Clean hands and pure hearts are necessary preconditions for knowing God. Therefore, spirit is something that can be spotless or stained, clean or unclean, acceptable or

---

[11] Psalm 51.

[12] Psalm 51:7.

[13] Matthew 5:8.

[14] See Soren Kierkegaard, *Purity of Heart Is to Will One Thing* (New York: HarperOne, 1994).

unacceptable to God. *If you want to ascend the hill of the Lord to experience God's holy presence, clean hands and a pure heart are needed.*[15]

Jesus gave his disciples a dwelling presence-metaphor when he said, "Remain in me, and I will remain in you."[16] We can be said to dwell with Jesus if we are branches, connected to him who is the True Vine. To be out of Jesus' influence is to become disconnected from the vine, possibly to attaching oneself to other sources for sustenance. The human spirit can attach itself to God, or be detached from God's presence. Disconnected people will not experience God. *To be in the presence of God is to be attached to him, and acquire one's life-resources from him.*

Scripture presents God as "our fortress and strength."[17] Metaphorically, God is a "house," within which he resides. When we live within the walls of God's protective fortress, "what shall we fear?" Thus, Henri Nouwen asks the question, "Is your experience of the house of God, or the house of fear?"[18]

It is in God's house, God's presence, that our spirits find comfort, encouragement, and strength for the journey. When we dwell outside these protective walls, and life's attacks come, fear and anxiety predominate. Our spirit is said to have a home. We are endangered when we make our home anything but God. *To abide in the fortress of God is to live in, and thus experience, the presence of God.*

Scripture provides several spatial metaphors of God's presence. These presence-metaphors indicate the "location" of spirit. For example, Jesus said, "But when you pray, go into your room, close the door and pray to your Father, who is unseen."[19] This "upper room," or "secret place," is a

---

[15] Psalm 24:3-4 – "Who may ascend the mountain of the LORD? Who may stand in his holy place? The one who has clean hands and a pure heart."

[16] John 15:4.

[17] Psalm 59:8-9

[18] See Henri Nouwen, *Lifesigns: Intimacy, Fecundity, and Ecstasy in Christian Perspective* (New York: Image, 1989).

[19] Matthew 6:6.

heart where Jesus presents himself. Our heart is allowed to be Christ's home. As the old hymn asks, "Have You Any Room for Jesus?" But our "rooms" can be "cluttered," leaving no space for God. The human spirit is a roomy space that either accommodates God's presence, or shuts God out. *God has created us with hearts designed for his occupation.*

One more example of a biblical presence-metaphor is: *the human heart is a temple.* This spatial metaphor describes the heart as a building that God occupies, and in which God can be known in the sense of encountered. The apostle Paul tells the Corinthians that they are, individually and corporately, temples of God's Holy Spirit.[20] That is, they host, within themselves, the presence of God. Our spirit is a holy place where God's Spirit dwells. To be "spiritual" is to allow God to reign, presently, in one's spirit, which is God's rightful dwelling place. To be "unspiritual" is to occupy this inner sanctuary with our own ego as king, while painting the outside to appear to be presence-driven.

We could take a long, slow boat ride through Scripture and identify countless examples of the presence motif. In a way, Gordon Fee has done this in his monumental book *God's Empowering Presence.*[21] The sheer plentitude of presence passages strengthens my case for the centrality of the presence motif in Scripture.

The above examples tell us three things. First, they figuratively define what it means to be in the presence of God. Second, they present being in God's presence as the greatest thing. Third, they tell us that we access and encounter God as we:

- Surrender to God.
- Anchor ourselves to God.
- Are whole-hearted towards God.
- Tend the fire within.
- Remain clean before God.

---

[20] I Corinthians 3:16; 6:19.
[21] Gordon Fee, *God's Empowering Presence* (Grand Rapids: Baker, 2009).

Attach ourselves to God.
- Dwell in God's fortress.
- Make room in our heart for God.
- Walk in holiness.[22]

Fee writes, "For Paul the Spirit, as an experienced and living reality, was the absolutely crucial matter for Christian life, from beginning to end."[23] This is about the manifest, tangible presence of God's Spirit, not some theoretical understanding about God.

The presence motif is core Judeo-Christianity. Which means, again: It really is all about God. God really is what we need. "God with us" defines the reality of where we come from, what our ultimate destiny is, what we long for, and what we most need.

The good news, the amazing truth, is that God's guiding presence is available to us. This, according to Dallas Willard, is the "good news." Jesus' "good news was about the availability of the kingdom of God."[24]

God *desires to,* and *is capable of,* leading the Church. God wants to "go before us." We, then, are to follow after God. This is the presence motif applied to leadership. This is the "without which" Moses says, "Then I'm not going."

---

[22] When we reverse these presence metaphors we see that we dwell out of God's presence as our hearts are:

...noisy
...restless
...fragmented/divided
...cluttered
...white-washed
...stained (by sin)
...disconnected from the Vine
...dwelling out God's fortress.
...and so on...

[23] Fee, *God's Empowering Presence*, p. 1.

[24] Dallas Willard and Gary Moon, *Eternal Living: Reflections on Dallas Willard's Teaching on Faith and Formation* (Downers Grove: InterVarsity Press, 2015), Kindle Location 2258.

The presence motif assumes that God, presently, is doing something. A kingdom is emerging in Real Church. God is the Chief Architect of this. God is the Builder, and *desires* to be such. It is important to acknowledge this, because "unless the Lord build the house, those who build it labor in vain."[25]

God wants to build his house. Our role is to co-labor with all that God is constructing. This is where we come in. God is using people to bring in his kingdom. We are, individually and collectively, living stones, being brick-and-mortared into God's Temple.

God *is capable of* leading Church. As all-knowing, God knows more about building than we do. As all-powerful, God is not limited, as we are. God is supremely *able*; we are shackled with *inability*.

God has an impressive resume that includes vast job experience. God has transcendent causal and intellectual capabilities. It makes sense that we allow the Holy Spirit to lead us.

This is the role of the Spirit. Gordon Fee writes:

> "The Holy Spirit is none other than the fulfillment of the promise that God himself would once again be present with his people... The Spirit is God's own personal presence in our lives and in our midst; he leads us into paths of righteousness for his name's sake, he "is working all things in all people," he is grieved when his people do not reflect his character and thus reveal his glory..., and he is present in our worship, as we sing "praise and honor and glory and power" to God and to the Lamb."[26]

This is the presence motif. It is the interpretive key to the book of Exodus. In Exodus, the people are seeking for the experiential presence of God. They follow God's tangible presence through the wilderness. Moses wanted to

---

[25] Ps. 127:1.
[26] Fee, *God's Empowering Presence* (Grand Rapids: Baker, 2007).

camp out near the tabernacle, because that was where God was localizing his omnipresence.[27]

At Redeemer we sing a worship song that has the line, "I want to be where You are." Being where God is produces belief. It is one thing to theoretically talk *about* God and his love and power; it is quite another thing to *encounter and experience the Living God.* This encounter and experience is the desire of nations.

The presence motif gains strength in the New Testament. The Jesus-story has always been about this. Knowing Scripture is good, but it is far from enough. Scripture is intended to bring us into a living, knowing and being-known, relationship with God. What people need is the real presence of God, not a theory or doctrine about it. This is precisely what Dallas Willard says the Gospel offers us; viz., the availability of the rule and reign of God.

Things like God's love, grace, and mercy are nothing if not experiential realities of the God who is with us. We are told that the Holy Spirit deluges our hearts with such things. As Paul testifies in Romans 5:5, "hope does not put us to shame, because God's love has been poured out into our hearts through the Holy Spirit, who has been given to us."

God's beautiful and fearful presence is in the garden in Genesis I, and the final knee-buckling chapters of Revelation. It is in the Psalmist doorkeeper's desire, and the Pauline "in Christ." Moses refuses to move without it. Jesus tells his disciples to primordially abide in it. This is the world's promised "Emmanuel, God with us."

Do not mistake the presence of God for performance. It has nothing to do with entertainment. Instead of an audience voting thumbs up or thumbs

---

[27] In Exodus 33:I we read that Moses spent time in the portable sanctuary of God's presence, where God "used to speak to Moses face to face."

down on what they thought of the church "service," faces and thumbs are on the ground before our holy God.[28]

To know this earth-shattering presence, one must be stripped and restored, like a piece of wood undergoing sandpaper and knife. Ruth Haley Barton writes:

> "It takes profound willingness to invite God to search us and know us at the deepest level of our being, allowing him to show us the difference between the performance-oriented drivenness of the false self and the deeper calling to lead from our authentic self in God. There is an elemental chaos that gets stirred up when we have been in God's presence enough that we can recognize pretense and performance and every other thing that bolsters our sense of self. It is unnerving to see evidence that these patterns are still at work—perhaps just a bit more subtly—in our everyday lives."[29]

My claim in this chapter is this: The origin, meaning, purpose, and destiny of the entire creation is about being with God. Christianity's great truth is that God has come to take up residence with us. God comes to "make his home in us."[30] Dallas Willard writes: "God is able to penetrate and intertwine himself within the fibers of the human self in such a way that those who are enveloped in his loving companionship will never be alone."[31]

My counter-claim is this: Life's most devastating thing is to dwell outside of God's presence. Any church that has lost sight of this has lost its identity and its reason for being.

---

[28] Sadly, many come to church to be "serviced."

[29] Ruth Haley Barton, *Strengthening the Soul of Your Leadership* (Downers Grove: InterVarsity, 2008), p. 126.

[30] John 14:23.

[31] Dallas Willard, *Hearing God: Developing a Conversational Relationship with God* (Downers Grove: InterVarsity, 2012), p. 59

We need more than what the ideas of people can give us. We need God, presently.

With us.

Our people don't need great sermons or great music; they need a great God. Thinking and learning about God is cool, but the idea all along has been "Emmanuel," *God with us.* As Leonard Ravenhill once said, "You can have all of your doctrines right—yet still not have the presence of God."[32]

It's true that God's presence can be mediated through preaching and worship. But, as people leave the sanctuary on a Sunday morning, we know the real thing has happened if they say, not, "What great preaching," and not, "What an awesome worship band," but rather, "What a great God!"

James McDonald writes:

> "God's provision for all that we need is His manifest presence with us. God doesn't dispense strength, wisdom, or comfort like a druggist fills a prescription; He promises us Himself— His manifest presence with us, as all that we will ever need— as enough! We must be terrified at the thought of a single step without it, without the Lord."[33]

---

[32] Brown, Michael L.. *Authentic Fire: A Response to John MacArthur's Strange Fire* (Lake Mary, Florida: Creation House, 2015), p. 293.
[33] James McDonald, *Vertical Church: What Every Heart Longs For, What Every Church Can Be,* Kindle Locations 934-937.

Years ago I wrote a worship song called "Manifest Presence."[34] We sing it, occasionally, at Redeemer. Songs like this focus us on the presence motif. When people are caught up in the river of God's presence you won't have to advertise it, because you don't have to advertise a flood. As Howard Thurman once said, *everything is available in God's presence.*

LEADERSHIP STEPS AND SUGGESTIONS

Decide, among your leaders, whether or not the presence motif is the river running through Scripture, and into which all other tributaries flow. Agree, or disagree?

True or false: Church really is all about God. If this is true, then what are the implications for us, as leaders of our people?

Preach, and teach, on the presence motif. *Develop and present, over time, a slow-cooked, simmering, biblical case for the presence motif.* Take it slow. Be led by God. God can show you the when and how, as it fits with your Jesus-community.

Draw attention to signs and stories in your Church that are evidence of God's presence. Allow for your people to share testimonies of their experiences with God.

---

[34] *MANIFEST PRESENCE (John Piippo)*
You are the Lord my God, Israel's creator, my K ing
Maker of heaven and earth
Lord God almighty, now I sing
Come do a new thing Lord I am finally ready, my soft heart is ready
I'm chasing after You, God
Your signs and wonders, mystery and power
Let Your manifest presence Fall like glory
Fill this temple With awe and wonder
Make a way in the desert
Streams in the wasteland
New wine in my heart
Spirit, let it come, Let it fall

4

PRESENCE COMES BEFORE PURPOSE AND PROGRAMS

In the movie "Field of Dreams" we heard words that have become immortalized, even theologized. "If you build it, he will come."

The movie was about a son who felt called to build a baseball diamond in the middle of an Iowa cornfield, in the hope that his father would return from the dead and play ball with him. When the father finally emerges through the corn rows and plays catch with his son, tears came to my eyes. What a scene! I could not help but think of my dad, playing ball with me, in the park adjacent to our house.

As beautiful as that scene is, there is no analogy between the movie and the father's appearance, and the kingdom of God and God's appearance. It is not true that, "If you build it [something, whatever], then God will come."

But the following is true: *When God comes, he will build it.* This, also, is true: *When God comes and tells you to build, then build.* The order is this.

First, God comes. Second, God builds.

What God builds is his kingdom. Jesus-followers are invited to join in the construction. When God shows up, he and you will build together.

In this chapter I argue that accessing God's presence comes before doing something. The Presence is before the edifice.

Do not build without hearing from God first. Do not assume what you are constructing in your church is something God intends to inhabit. Do not make the mistake that structure, by itself, brings life.

I have seen, and been part of, church programs that burn people and pastors out. This is rampant in the American church.[1] Resolve to no longer partake in this. Refuse to spend time in meetings, thinking up programs, recruiting people to service them, in the hope that the programs will be life-giving, and then organizing and administrating those programs with the expectation that God is pleased.[2]

One difference between presence-drivenness and program-drivenness is this: when the former happens, people burn; when the latter happens, people burn out.

The fire comes before the program. The fire must be tended. Here is where hard work and administration come in. But God is still Shepherd of the whole thing. Scripture tells us that, unless God builds the house, we labor in vain.[3] It is not the case that, if *we* build physical structures, God is obligated to come and bless them with his presence. Laboring in vain is the water that quenches the flickering flame.

Presence-driven leaders understand that God is the architect, not us. God is constructing a spiritual temple for his habitation. Do not build without God's counsel. To ensure this, pastors and people must connect to God,

---

[1] It has been my privilege, since 1977, to instruct three to four thousand pastors and Christian leaders in the spiritual life. This includes teaching at several seminaries, speaking at pastors' conferences and retreats, and churches. Many are burned out as a result of doing, without being.

[2] This observation is at the heart of Francis Chan's decision to leave his megachurch. See *The Christian Post*, June 29, 2017.

[3] Psalm 127:1 — *Unless the LORD builds the house, the builders labor in vain.*

like a branch connects to a vine. Using another biblical metaphor, we must be "built in" to Christ so that we "align" with him.[4]

Paul's counsel in I Corinthians is instructive here. God, through Paul (who functioned as a contractor), laid a foundation for Church. The chief cornerstone of that foundation is Christ crucified.

The superstructure is made of people. Paul uses "temple" language to describe it (precious stones, jewels, etc., things that adorned Solomon's Temple). Instead of being a physical temple, this new temple is made of people. Now *you* are a temple of the Holy Spirit.

A temple is a structure that houses and hosts the presence of God. God is a builder, and is building a people whom he will inhabit, with his Spirit, and for his praise. He comes to take up residence in us.

As this happens, we experience life. Where there is life, we build structure.[5]

For example, God told several of us at Redeemer that we were to assist the kingdom-building he was doing in Bangkok, through NightLight International. NightLight is a Christian organization dedicated to setting victims of global sex trafficking free.[6] Once we discerned this was God calling us to build, we began to work. We organized and administrated, as God led us to partner with NightLight. Our corporate experience was bursting with fire and life! We didn't have to fund-raise. Financial gifts came in as God's calling was felt by our people.[7]

To some, organization and administration might seem boring. This is not the case for people who organize for a great cause God has called them to. Administration is a Spirit-empowered gift, mentioned in I Corinthians 12:28. The root meaning of "administrate" is to govern, pilot, direct, or

---

[4] I Peter 2:4-6.

[5] Where the fire of God is, tend it. In doing this we host the presence of God.

[6] nightlightinternational.com.

[7] Now, many years later, the financial gifts are still coming in for NightLight.

steer, a ship.[8] The directions of where to steer the ship come out of God's presence. In God's kingdom, even organization and administration are presence-driven activities.

I have a friend, Joe, who has greatly influenced me. Joe loves to work in his large vegetable and flower garden. He feels called to do this. Joe talks about needing "garden time." He tills and sows, waters and weeds, trims and prunes, throughout the hot summer days. In late summer and early fall, he reaps the joy of his vegetables, fruits, and flowers. Some of them have overflowed onto Linda and me. I say to him, "That's your therapy." Blessed is the one whose garden bears much fruit.

Working with a fruit-bearing purpose brings Joe great satisfaction. It is the same in life. Where does life purpose come from? It comes from God, and is revealed as we dwell in God's presence. In his presence, God directs our paths. He calls us to do things. *In terms of order, intimacy with God in his presence is prior to whatever plans and purposes he has for us.*

Purpose comes out of prayerfulness. In prayer, one hears the call of God to "Go," or "Do." Famously, *doing* is an emergent property of *being*. What we do is a co-laboring with God and his purposes. Therefore, *we connect with God before we act.*

This is the heart of true prayer, which is: talking with God about what we (God and I) are thinking and doing together.[9] Like Joe and his fall harvest, I want to come to the end of my life knowing God has worked through me to accomplish his desires. I want my life to bear fruit that will last in the hearts of people. That is not only good, but is therapy for my soul. Meaningful doing is the antidote to boredom. The meaning of what we are doing is experienced in the presence of God.

---

[8] The Greek word is *kybernesis*. This word has a root meaning of to steer a ship, to guide. See William Mounce - https://billmounce.com/greek-dictionary/kybernesis.

[9] I have expanded on this in my book *Praying: Reflections on 40 Years of Solitary Conversations with God* (Bloomington, Indiana: Westbow, 2016).

LEADING THE PRESENCE-DRIVEN CHURCH | 43

The bleak ecclesiastical alternative is grinding out church work without spending time cultivating the garden of God's presence. This is labor without purpose, which produces a life of boring, meaningless anomie.[10] "Boredom" is not having nothing to do; boredom is finding no meaning and purpose in what you are doing. Presence should always come before production.

The call to our work, its purpose and *raison d'être*, must be grounded in life lived in God's presence. This is a *vocation*, not a "job," "career," or "occupation." Meaning and purpose emerge from hearing the voice (*voce*) of God. What must primarily occupy us is God.

Thomas Merton is helpful here. He writes:

> "Work occupies the body and the mind and is necessary for the health of the spirit. Work can help us to pray and be recollected, *if we work properly*. Agitation, however, destroys the spiritual usefulness of work and even tends to frustrate its physical and social purpose. Agitation is the useless and ill-directed action of the body. It expresses the inner confusion of a soul without peace."[11]

The "proper work" Merton refers to is work assigned by God, for God's great purposes. Otherwise, our labor is "useless and ill-directed"; or, more accurately, non-directed. As we live lives abiding in God's presence, our work will be relevant, and have its place in the economy of God's kingdom.

Thus, we are to first abide in Jesus. Let him shepherd our soul. A little bit of churchgoing won't help. Constant abiding will. Out of this Christ-dwelling comes not only his peace and joy, but life purpose.

---

[10] Anomie (from https://www.britannica.com/topic/anomie): a condition of instability resulting from a breakdown of standards and values or from a lack of purpose or ideals.
[11] Merton, *No Man Is an Island* (New York: Harcourt, 1982), pp. 114-115. Emphasis mine.

THE HOLY SPIRIT CANNOT BE PROGRAMMED.

My argument in this chapter is this: A presence-driven church must

1) Seek God first.
2) Discern what God wants you to do.
3) Then, do it.

The seeking and discerning happen in the presence of God. Being-with God undergirds doing-with God.

When church programming exceeds being in God's presence, *doing* overwhelms *being*. When people are burned out with all the doing, being with God is the loser. When this happens *we* are leading, not God.

God's primary call is to love him, not do things. Doing things out of obedience is a way of loving God. But God does not call us to do things, just for the sake of doing them. Don't "do" without first being directed by God. True-north direction comes from God, and is discerned by accessing God's presence.

God's doings will look different than our ideas. Jesus's way of doing things, to include how he rescues and redeems humanity, consistently confounded the disciples and religious leaders. Therefore, practicing the presence of God must come before doing things. The being of God is not the doings of humanity. God's ways are not my ways.

We cannot program or predict how the Holy Spirit will lead us. God is infinitely more creative than we are. God's Spirit will not be boxed in by our limitations. To recognize that God is God, and I am not, means that on Sunday mornings we have some things in place - an opening worship song, we pray for our children, announcements (if any), praise & worship, preaching, then a time of ministry. But all this can, and often does, change, as the Spirit directs. My experience is that, in a presence-driven church, change will be common, and *vive la difference* is celebrated.

Recently, as our church family was worshiping on a Sunday morning, one of our men, Jason, came to me and said, "I believe we are to take an offering for Aloysious." Aloysious is from Uganda. He began a children's school there, and was in the United States visiting some friends. One of them invited him to Redeemer. We were honored to have him with us.

I introduced him, shared the impoverished conditions he had come out of, and how God was using him in the development of a school for children. When Jason came to me, I thought, "That is right! This is what God is now doing." God was orchestrating our worship service. God was directing us. I have come to see this as more exciting and life-giving than whatever I come up with. We took an offering for Aloysious, even though this was not "in the program." It was beautiful to see many people bringing their gifts to the altar, and placing them in a basket.

On Sunday mornings we begin with a simple, basic structure. That's OK, and, I think, good. But within this structure there is breathing room for God to lead. And he does. He directs our paths, even on Sunday mornings. Presence-driven leaders become familiar with this. Presence-driven people like it when God directs their paths.

We do not have an "order of service," or "program," to be strictly followed. While God can, and does, pre-order what happens in our corporate gatherings, it is *God*, not myself or a committee, doing the pre-ordering. God's Spirit will not be boxed in by our cognitive limitations.

To program God is to suppress him. Pastorally, that is the *worst* place to be. Remember how Jesus shut down the Temple because the religious leaders "shut the door of the kingdom of heaven in people's faces." Jesus said, "You yourselves do not enter, nor will you let those enter who are trying to."[12]

Programming that does not emerge out of deep abiding in Christ puts God in a box. This caused A.W. Tozer to look on American churches in dismay. Writing in 1948, Tozer said:

---

[12] Matthew 23:13.

"I wonder if there was ever a time when true spiritual worship was at a lower ebb. To great sections of the Church the art of worship has been lost entirely, and in its place has come that strange and foreign thing called the 'program.' This word has been borrowed from the stage, and applied with sad wisdom to the type of public service which now passes for worship among us."[13]

The Holy Spirit is unpredictable and non-programmable. The Spirit cannot be ordered. A presence-driven church will move with the Spirit into places we do not control. The Spirit's leading is for building God's kingdom, for his name's sake, and not for our need to keep control of things.

PRESENCE-LESS PROGRAMMING DEVOLVES INTO ENTERTAINMENT

I was twenty years old, and leading Sunday morning worship in a Lutheran Church on the campus of Northern Illinois University. I would arrive for the morning service after a long night of drinking, drugs, and partying. Being a good guitar player who was accustomed to playing drunk, I was able to pull it off.

I could play better drunk than many worship leaders could play straight. They paid me ten dollars a Sunday to do this. No one asked about my spiritual life. They needed a worship leader, and I was a warm body. I did it, though I was far from Christ, and could care less about God.

I can't remember how I got this gig, who asked me, and why I was never questioned about my spiritual condition. I had never led worship in my life! I never worshiped God. I knew nothing about God's presence. But, I was good for the program. The show must go on. After all, we don't want to bore the people!

---

[13] A. W. Tozer, *The Pursuit of God* (New York: Christian Miracle Foundation Press), Kindle Locations 46-51.

I was a musician filling a perceived need. Since then, I have discovered this is not unusual in the Entertainment Church.[14]

How important is musical skill in worship leading, or playing on a worship team? My answer is: not much. My standards for our worship musicians are these:

1) You must be yourself a worshiper who seeks and loves God's presence.
2) You must be able to play well enough so as not to distract people from worshiping. If your guitar playing is hideous, people will be drawn to the discordant carnage more than to God. On your instrument, be adequate. Take that part seriously. Get lessons and grow.

As important as musicianship is, living a life of consistent, passionate, Christ-abiding is more important. Instrumental ability without a Christ-formed heart creates "performance," without God-presence.

This is important, because *worship is all about God's presence*. Real worship is corporate God-directedness. Worship is movement within the temple of God. If the God-movement is not in the hearts of the worship leaders, great instrumental ability shuts the door to true adoration of God by sending the wrong message ("How Great Is Our Guitar Player").

Once again, A.W. Tozer speaks from beyond the grave. In *The Root of the Righteous* he has a chapter entitled, "The Presence More Important Than the Program." He writes:

> "When we compare our present carefully programmed meetings with the New Testament we are reminded of the remark of a famous literary critic after he had read

---

[14] I have heard many stories of musicians who told me they were asked to fill in on some church's worship band, even though they were engaged in illicit sex, on drugs, and basically uninterested in anything that was religious.

Alexander Pope's translation of Homer's Odyssey: He said - "It is a beautiful poem, but it is not Homer."

The fast-paced, highly spiced, entertaining [church] service of today may be a beautiful example of masterful programming— but it is not a Christian service. The two are leagues apart in almost every essential. About the only thing they have in common is the presence of a number of persons in one room. There the similarity ends and glaring dissimilarities begin. For one thing, the object of attention is not the same in the two meetings."[15]

A program-driven church is not a Christian church. Is that too strong? Some say it is not strong enough. Eugene Peterson has written that *a Consumer Church is an AntiChrist Church.* How so? For the following reasons.[16]

- The ways Jesus goes about loving and saving the world are personal. The ways our North American culture uses are impersonal.
- In churches today the vocabulary of numbers is preferred over names. A "number" is an impersonal abstract object; a person is flesh-blood-and-spirit being created in God's image.
- The Real Jesus is an alternative to the dominant ways of the world, not a supplement to them; e.g., to make us happy and meet our individual needs.
- The Consumer Church replaces the Jesus way with the American way.
- The American consumer mentality runs so deep that many churches unreflectively replicate it. The implicit, unconscious reasoning is this: In America we are the world's champion consumers, so why shouldn't we have state-of-the-art consumer churches? This is the best and most effective way for gathering large and prosperous congregations.

---

[15] A. W. Tozer, *The Root of the Righteous* (Camp Hill, PA: Wing Spread Publishers, 1986), Kindle Location 910.

[16] See Eugene Peterson, *The Jesus Way: A Conversation on the Ways That Jesus Is the Way* (Grand Rapids: Eerdmans, 2007).

- We can't gather a God-fearing, God-worshiping congregation by cultivating a consumer-pleasing, commodity-oriented congregation.
- American Christianity is known for going along with whatever culture decides is charismatic, successful, influential - whatever gets things done, whatever can gather a crowd of followers - hardly noticing that these ways and means are at odds with the clearly marked way that Jesus walked and called us to follow. American churches are largely dictated to by American culture. Here is where "relevant" becomes a bad idea.

Peterson concludes: "The ways and means promoted and practiced in the world are a systematic attempt to substitute human sovereignty for God's rule. The world as such has no interest in following the crucified King."[17]

A church may have awesome music and crowd-attracting programs, but be void of God's presence. This happens when the focus is on the awesome musicians and programs, some of which may display little or no knowledge of the God they presume to play before. When that happens, a church has lost its reason for being.

I would like to take a time machine and go back to the first century, into the world of the first church meeting in that upper room, before and after Pentecost. How was the worship? They didn't have a band, yet in Acts 2 we are told they spent time praising God.[18] Paul tells us the early church meetings included singing "psalms and hymns and spiritual songs among yourselves, singing and making melody to the Lord in your hearts."[19] How cool was the music? Did the people like the worship? Those are the wrong questions. The correct questions are, did they experience God's presence? Did the people worship? The answers are yes Lord, yes Lord, yes, yes, Lord![20]

---

[17] Ib.

[18] Acts 2:46-47.

[19] Ephesians 5:19. See also Colossians 3:16.

[20] Hebraic worship, and early Christian worship, was repetitive. See http://www.johnpiippo.com/2011/09/we-need-more-repetitive-worship-tribal.html.

When people return to the heart of worship, they realize following Jesus is radically different from following anyone else. At this point we have something distinctive, which the secular world cannot offer. Martyn Lloyd-Jones said, "When the church is absolutely different from the world, she invariably attracts it. It is then that the world is made to listen to her message, though it may hate it at first."[21]

Like most pastors, I don't want to be hated. I want to be attractive and appealing, to be liked, and friended on Facebook. This gets harder and harder as I get older and older. The desire to be awesome seduces me to focus on attracting more and more people. This tempts me to copy the world, since our consumer economy markets products in attractive packages. But if I am here to offer something distinctive, something the world cannot provide, why would I want to copy the world? What if the Church really is all about God and his presence? What if I am not the offering this world needs?

Church was always meant to be different from the world systems. Jesus said his kingdom was not of this world. The kingdom of heaven is an alternative kingdom. A different way of being and doing.

Real Church presents an alternative to our programmed world. The core distinctive of this beautiful kingdom is God himself, manifesting his weighty presence in the giving of spiritual gifts, producing his own character in people ("spiritual fruit"), setting captives free (healing and deliverance), and forming a people after his name.

Presence is more important than programming, even more important than entertaining. Presence is not about people pleasing. It's not even about meeting people's needs. Real Church is not a personal need-meeting machine.[22]

---

[21] Martyn Lloyd-Jones, *Studies In the Sermon on the Mount* (Grand Rapids: Eerdmans, 1958), p. 28.
[22] For some good stuff about this see James Van Yperen, *Making Peace: A Guide to Overcoming Church Conflict* (Chicago: Moody, 2002), pp. 29 ff.

The presence-driven church really is all about God with us, presently, in experience. I could never program what happened last Sunday with Jason and Aloysious. I couldn't predict it. It wasn't given to entertain us. There, emerging before our eyes, out of the tangible worship presence of God, came an Idea. A Word. It took on flesh, and dwelt among us. It seemed right, to us all. All we had to do was worship him, listen for his voice, and obey.

LEADERSHIP STEPS AND SUGGESTIONS

Pastors - develop and present the case for the primacy of God's presence, through sermons, classes, home groups, dialogues over coffee, etc.

Evaluate whether it has begun to take root in your people.

Are your people buying in to the idea that, above and before all else, we must be a people who dwell in God's presence?

Pay attention to thoughts, ideas, and leadings your people have as they focus on abiding in God's presence.

Take a sabbatical from "doing," and focus on abiding. Ask questions like, "What is God saying to you?" "What is God telling you to do?"

Listen to what God is saying to your people. Discern what is from God, and what is not.

As your people become an abiding people, expect that God will call them to action. Be prepared to listen and support them, even if it is not the way you would do things.

5

HOW TO EXPERIENCE GOD'S PRESENCE

When our sons were boys, I would return home from an afternoon of praying, approach our small house, and look through the living room window from the outside. I would see Linda, Dan, and Josh, playing a game together, or reading a book, just talking, or taking naps. I would think, "Everything I love most dearly is in this room, *now.*" I would pause, thank God for this window through time, and savor it to its depths.

Now.

Presently.

These are *kairos* moments, now-encounters with God.[1]

Kairos is the biblical Greek word for "God's time," as in "the appointed time."[2] The Greek word for ordinary clock time is *chronos*. Think of the ticking time piece on the TV show "60 Minutes." That's *chronos*. God's

---

[1] For how difficult it is, in physics, to understand what "now" is, see *Now: The Physics of Time*, by Richard Muller (New York: W.W. Norton, 2016).

[2] For example, Matthew 26:18; Luke 1:20.

presence runs on *kairos*, not *chronos*.[3] Kairos moments are periods of extended timelessness. In a sense, one feels that time has stopped.

How do we experience God's presence? The answer is simple, as it should be. Go to the Temple. In ancient Israel, *to experience God's presence, go to the Temple in Jerusalem.* For disciples of Jesus, *to experience God's presence, abide in Christ.* Now, we are the Temple that hosts the presence of God.

How do we abide in Christ? To abide in Christ, engage in spiritual disciplines.[4] Spiritual disciplines attach us to God. This connection is possible now, in the present moment. In this chapter, I am going to share my understanding of this.

TO EXPERIENCE GOD'S PRESENCE, ABIDE IN CHRIST

We have an old pear tree in our back yard. As I bite into one of these pears I tell Linda, "This is the fruit of the gods!" The pears grow on the branches. The branches are attached to the trunk of the tree. This connection allows the nutrients of the trunk to flow into the branches. To produce pears, the branch just needs to stay connected. It needs to remain, or abide, in the trunk of the tree.

To be, in the present moment, attached to Jesus is to *abide* in him. The word can be translated "to remain," or "to dwell." To dwell is to truly be with someone. "Abide" is an experiential word, describing a lingering, slow-cooked, togetherness.

The Greek word is *menon*. It has the sense of tarrying, hanging around, "to be kept continually." *Menon* is a *kairos* word. It connotes, "Slow down, spend

---

[3] See William Lane Craig on God as temporal in relation to the creation, and non-temporal without the creation. See Craig's essay "Timelessness and Omnitemporality"; and his book *Time and Eternity: Exploring God's Relationship to Time* (Wheaton, Illinois: Crossway, 2001).

[4] See especially Dallas Willard, *The Spirit of the Disciplines* (New York: HarperCollins, 1988); and Richard Foster, *Celebration of Discipline* (New York: HarperCollins, 1978).

the day with me. Kick off your shoes. Here's a cup of coffee. Let's recline in the fireplace room, and *be* together."

Menon is a being-word, more than a doing-word. It is a presence word. *Menon* is active, alert, focused, and engaged. It has the thickness and intensity of a lover, with their beloved.

To abide with someone is to full-being be with them, interact with them, and meet with them. It is to hang out together, with cell phones off and stowed away.

I had an abiding time last night. It was cold and clear where we live in Michigan. I told Linda, "I'm going out for a moment to look at the stars." I put on my warmest coat and hat. I slipped on my gloves. I stepped out the door to be with God. I walked around the house into our back yard, where it is darker. I looked up. And it happened, again, as it always does to me. I sensed God, with me.[5]

I thought, "Who am I, God, that you have me on your mind?" A soul-filling took place. My smallness was inhabited by God's vastness. I was simply being with God, for no other purpose than to be with him.

Be with God for the sole purpose of being with God. Like a lover with her beloved. This is the *telos*, or purpose, of life. This is how it will all end. Abiding in Christ now brings our destiny to us. We experience a foretaste of divine glory. This is experience as eschatology.

The foretaste occurs *now.* And again, and again, and again.

In the abiding life, I experience many "nows" with God. Underline the word 'this' in Psalm 118:24, which says, *This is the day that the LORD has made; let us rejoice and be glad in it.* Presently.

---

[5] Within my worldview, this kind of experience transcends mere Einsteinian wonder. I am standing before a creation, not a secular cosmos.

In John 15, Jesus instructs his disciples to "abide in him," as their first order of being. Before they get busy and do things, they are to get busy *being someone*, in relationship, with him. This is because "in him we live and move and have our being."[6] This is because, without him, all our activity is worthless chaff. Jesus said if we are disconnected from him, we do nothing. We have a choice between a fruitful life of abiding, or a barren life of disconnection.

Abiding in Christ happens in the present. Being absorbed by the past or future causes us to miss the wonder of now. As Greg Boyd has said, "God is the great "I AM," not the great "I was" or the great "I will be.""[7]

Jesus's command for us to abide in him is in sync with the Great Commandment to love God with all we are. Abiding in Christ is the main way of engaging in this love relationship. As we abide, ongoingly, in God's presence, we are loving God for who he is, not for what he can do for us.

This is intimacy with God, in a way the ancient Hebrews did not know, but was promised to them. "One day," God said, "I will put my Spirit in you."[8] "One day, I will flood you with my Spirit."[9] This promise was seen in the Psalms. A day is coming, when "the devout worshiper could be assured of God's presence and love in any geographical location. This in turn gave birth to a sense that the living God would come to dwell, not just within the Temple, but within the worshipers themselves."[10]

To abide in Christ is to reify our status and identity.[11] This is seen in Paul's identity-status term, "in Christ." In his letters, he uses "in Christ" (with variations) two hundred and sixteen times.[12] This sums up our union, and

---

[6] Acts 17:28.

[7] Greg Boyd, *Present Perfect: Finding God in the Now* (Grand Rapids: Zondervan, 2010).

[8] Ezekiel 26:27; 37:14.

[9] Acts 2:17.

[10] N. T. Wright, *The Case for the Psalms: Why They Are Essential* (New York: HarperCollins, 2013), p. 114. See chapter four in its entirety – "Where God Dwells."

[11] To reify is to make something that is abstract more concrete and real.

[12] Michael Parsons, "'In Christ' in Paul." https://biblicalstudies.org.uk/pdf/vox/vol18/in-christ_parsons.pdf.

intimacy, with Christ. It is Christ's presence, the "hope of glory," in every follower of Jesus. The Pauline "in Christ" "primarily designates a close and indissoluble relationship with the Lord."[13]

To discover our "in Christ" identity is to deepen our experience with God. To realize this is, as Frank Laubach said,

> "The most wonderful discovery of all... to use the words of Paul, "Christ liveth in me." He dwells in us, walks in our minds, reaches out through our hands, speaks with our voices, if we respond to His every whisper."[14]

When we live "in Christ," otherwise trivial moments are transformed into Kingdom experiences. This is because we are allowing God to reign over the present moment.[15]

As we abide, Christ reigns in us. God rules in our present moment, as we attach to him. In abiding times, we are led into what God wants us to do. Out of the abiding relationship comes life's directives. As we trust and obey, our experience of God deepens. This is what it means to say that our *doing* comes from our *being*.

In being branchlike, we experience life that bears much lasting "fruit."[16] We do things Jesus did, and even greater things. As we remain in Christ, like a pear branch connected to a pear tree, we receive the resources of the roots, to include peace and joy. This peace and joy is unlike anything our world can give us. It flows from God's Trinitarian being, into us, as connected branches.

All this is experiential. *To experience God, abide in Christ.*

---

[13] Parsons, Ib.

[14] In Boyd, Present Perfect, p. 118.

[15] See Ib., p. 125.

[16] John 15:8.

To abide in Christ is to be empowered by God's Spirit. Supernatural empowerment flows through us to do things, even greater things, than Jesus did.

Dwelling in Christ, we experience a love like no other. It is the love between Father, Son, and Spirit. As we are *in him*, we share the love that *is him*.

In him.

'In' is a container metaphor.[17] I am now writing *in* a room at the college where I teach. Thus, I share whatever atmosphere the room has. I see what is in the room. I hear the sounds of the room. "In" is an intimate word. As I go *out* of the room, I become detached, and fail to share in whatever gifts and benefits the room has for me.

To be *in* Christ is, metaphorically, dwelling in a room where the Father, Son, and Holy Spirit *are the room. The Trinitarian being of God is the space I am dwelling in.* I am *in him.*

With this, the ancient reality of being in God's presence is taken to a transcendent level. To be in Christ is to share the Trinitarian atmosphere. This is closer than "up close and personal." We most experience the presence of God when we abide in him.

Abiding is a type of trusting. I bought a new chair for my home office. I had the previous chair for twenty years. I trusted it. I knew it would hold me. Therefore, I had no anxiety about it. It would be contradictory to say, "I trust the chair I'm sitting in, but am afraid it won't hold me."

---

[17] 'In' is an ontological metaphor. See the most influential theory of metaphor in the past one hundred years, George Lakoff's and Mark Johnson's *Metaphors We Live By* (Chicago: University of Chicago Press, 1980). Here Lakoff and Johnson present their conceptual theory of metaphor. See also John Piippo, *Metaphor and Theology: A Multidisciplinary Approach* (PhD thesis, Northwestern University, 1986).

To abide in Christ is to trust him. I "put my trust in the Lord." Which means,

> If God was a chef, I would eat his cooking.
> If God was a shepherd, I would listen for his voice and follow.
> If God was a rock, I would stand on him.
> If God was a fortress, I would make my home in him.
> If God was a river, and I a tree, I would send my roots to him.
> If God was a vine, and I a branch, I would attach myself to him.
> If God was a fire, I would be consumed by him.
> If God was water, I would drink of him.
> If I was a cup, I would be filled to overflowing by him.
> If God was a hidden treasure, I would seek him.
> If God was a word, I would read him.
> If God was my Lord, I would obey him.
> If God was a chair, I would sit on him.

I would do these things every day... after day... after day.

There is a cumulative effect that results from a lifetime of trusting in God. A psychological confidence, a certitude, emerges. It is like the confidence I had because of sitting in the same chair for twenty years, and finding that, *through it all, it still holds.*

In this chapter I am sharing how we experience the presence of God. My answer is: we experience God's presence by abiding in Christ. This abiding, and trusting, is experiential. Gary Moon says the notion of the reality of experiencing God was the "golden thread" running through the theology of Dallas Willard. Moon writes:

> "I believe that if one were asked to identify a single golden thread that runs through each of Dallas Willard's books—a key idea that sets his thinking apart from so many others—it would be the idea that *it is actually possible*

to step into the words of John 17:3 and enter into an experiential relationship, a transforming friendship, with the Trinity. In the words of Steve Porter, an ordinary person can grab hold of life from above. An ordinary person can live a "with-God" life—surrendered and obedient to divine will."[18]

How, then, do we experience the presence of God?

First, none of this is about striving or trying harder. Once connected, the pear branch does not have to work at being fruitful. It *will* produce pears, inexorably, as a consequence of its attachment.

Second, discipline yourself spiritually. Attach yourself. Trust. The result of over four decades of spiritual discipline, for me, is that what was once a choice is now a habit.[19] The formation of habitual abiding *is* the transformation of the heart into increasing Christlikeness. This is God's presence, as a constant spiritual reality.

I choose to pray, worship, meditate on Scripture, serve, follow, and be in community. These are all ways of being in Christ. The result is that I know God, and experience God's presence.

Presence-driven leaders do this, as their first order of life. Presence-driven churches are communities of Christ-abiding people. Abiding in Christ is the platform from which all authentic and relevant ministry in the name of Jesus emerges. Without this, we do nothing.[20]

Finally, get still before the Lord. When our heart is still, our capacity for experiencing God elevates. Psalm 46:10 says, *Be still, and experience God.* I know your version of the Bible says, *Be still, and know that I am God.* But

[18] In Dallas Willard and Gary Moon, *Eternal Living: Reflections on Dallas Willard's Teaching on Faith and Formation* (Downers Grove: InterVarsity, 2015), Kindle Locations 292-294.
[19] See James K. A. Smith, *You Are What You Love: The Spiritual Power of Habit* (Grand Rapids: Brazos, 2016).
[20] John 15:5. Jesus tells his disciples, "Those who abide in me and I in them bear much fruit, because apart from me you can do nothing."

to understand this verse you must bracket your Western epistemological assumptions. Hebrew "knowing" is experiential, not merely theoretical. "Do you know how to jet ski?" means, "Can you do it? Have you experienced it? Has it happened to you?" Have you saddled up on a jet ski and trusted it?

We experience God's now-presence with us by stepping towards God and connecting. If there were a thousand steps between you and God, God takes 999 towards you. You take one step: abide. That brings connection.

ABIDING IN CHRIST IS NOT CONTINGENT ON SPACE OR TIME

Years ago, a friend of mine went to an isolated cabin in northern Ontario to get alone with God. His soul was a raging sea, and he needed to get away and spiritually calm the waters. He thought the sheer, quiet beauty of the lakes, rivers, and forests would assure experience of God's presence.

When he returned after a week alone, I asked how it went. He said, "Not good, because I brought my restless, troubled brain with me." In the hush of the deep forest the noise of his mind amplified, like tinnitus in a quiet bedroom. My friend's heart and mind were in a wrestling match.

You could be alone, in a cabin in the woods by a lake, with the breeze gentling blowing the autumn leaves, drinking fresh-brewed coffee and eating a warm cinnamon roll, and yet be noisy and cluttered within. The "be still" condition that results in experiencing God is non-environment, non-circumstance dependent. This is good news, because it means that God's presence can be experienced anywhere. It all depends on our heart.

I awoke at 6 AM this morning. I took my journal, and a devotional book by Howard Thurman, and sat on our deck. I read this:

> "One of these spiritual practices is the practice of silence,
> or quiet. I was accustomed to spend many hours alone
> in my rowboat, fishing along the river, where there was

no sound save the lapping of the waves against the boat...
There would come a moment when beyond the single pulse
beat there was a sense of Presence which seemed always to
speak to me. My response to the sense of Presence always
had the quality of personal communion. There was no
voice. There was no image. There was no vision. There
was God."[21]

Before presenting what a presence-driven church can look like, I have
shared what the experience of God's presence is like, and how it is accessed.
Experiencing God is a *kairos* event that happens presently, now. It is not
contingent on life's circumstances. Do not focus on making the experience
happen; focus on abiding in Christ. Utilize the spiritual disciplines. Learn
to be still before the Lord.

Live this way. As you do, your sense of the now-presence of God will increase.
It will be an everyday reality. You won't need to travel to special places to
encounter God more deeply. You will be living a presence-driven life.

LEADERSHIP APPLICATION

As a pastor or leader, make your primary focus abiding in Christ. Learn
and live a deeper abiding life in God's presence. Determine what spiritual
disciplines you will do, and step into them.

Invite your people to do the same. Teach them biblical ways of being and
staying connected to Christ. Coach your people in the spiritual disciplines.

Share your abiding experiences with others.

Teach John chapters 14-15 to your people.

---

[21] Howard Thurman, *40-Day Journey with Howard Thurman* (Minneapolis: Augsburg,
2009), p. 48

Teach the Pauline "in Christ" reality to your people, as a key to understanding the letters of Paul.

Continue to champion and make space for testimonies for your people, as they engage in the abiding life.

6

THE MARKS OF A PRESENCE-DRIVEN CHURCH

In 1970 a button was pushed, and I entered "Search me, O God" mode. This kickstarted forty-seven years of self-examination.

I'm with Socrates, who believed that the unexamined life is not worth living. My first spiritual mentors told me to constantly attend to my relationship with God.[1] I've done it, and it's given me a fair degree of self-knowledge. Of all persons I know, I know myself best. Even though imperfectly.

Of all churches I know, I know my church best. In this chapter I will tell you what I know about my church family, and how we are presence-driven. I will share the fruit of our presence-driven emphasis.

Your church may be presence-driven, and in some ways unlike ours. Nonetheless, there are core elements to a presence-driven church, without which it's a different kind of church.

I write of what I see and know. Some things are essential to any church that follows God's Spirit. Others are contingent, therefore non-essential. This will be true of any presence-driven church. There will be core elements, without which the church is not presence-driven. There will be unique

---

[1] See my book, *Praying: Reflections on 40 Years of Solitary Conversations with God.*

elements, signs of God's grace carved out specifically for such a church as yours. There will be common elements, shared by many churches.

My community, Redeemer Fellowship, was presence-driven before I arrived in 1992. The soil of Redeemer's soul had already been tilled and furrowed. The people were receptive and fertile to the leading of the Holy Spirit. I have learned much about presence-driven people since coming to Monroe. Hopefully, God has used me and Linda to add to the already-existing movement and growth.

Here are some of the ways the people of Redeemer Fellowship Church experience the presence motif.

WE TRAVEL WITHOUT A MAP

I tell my people that our lives should look like the maps of the apostle Paul. Paul never traveled in straight lines, from point A to point B. His routes zig-zagged, as he was led by the Holy Spirit. *The Presence-Driven Church zig-zags. It is Spirit-led, therefore unpredictable and non-programmable.*

We are like Abram, in Genesis 12:4: *So Abram went, as the LORD had told him; and Lot went with him.*

And from Hebrews 11:8: *By faith Abraham, when called to go to a place he would later receive as his inheritance, obeyed and went, even though he did not know where he was going.* Abraham did not know where he was going! How radical that is, when viewed from our obsessive goal-setting culture.

See how "God calls, and we go forth in faith without a map, not quite sure where we are going, but with trust in God's promised presence."[2] Abraham's only goal was to follow God.

---

[2] *Life With God Bible* (New York: HarperCollins, 2005), p. 32.

I like how Thomas Merton expresses this. He writes: "The real function of discipline is not to provide us with maps, but to sharpen our own sense of direction so that when we really get going we can travel without maps."[3]

Western culture, writes Adam Alter, is a "goal culture." Even though goals have been around forever, our goal culture is historically recent. This is related to "perfectionism" and, says Alter, "striving," like aiming for 20,000 steps on your Fitbit. When we travel without a map, striving diminishes because we are trusting in God's leading, rather than trying to reach some goal.[4] As our church is being led, we don't often know where we are going.

WE ARE LED, BEFORE WE LEAD

Do you like being led? Not everyone does. When my leader can be trusted, I have found it exhilarating, better than being in control.

When Linda and I went to Israel, Hal Ronning was our guide. Hal and his wife Mirja are great biblical scholars.[5] Hal knows the land of Israel like I know my backyard. He is a scholar of Semitic languages, and of the Bible.

Our tour met up with Hal in Tel Aviv. We got on the bus and headed north. I grabbed my notebook and pen, ready to take notes as Hal was talking. After a half hour of writer's cramp, I thought it best to forget the notes and just listen. Hal was a living historical and archaeological encyclopedia!

For ten days we followed Hal. It felt adventurous. My heart and head were overflowing with ideas and questions. Better that Hal lead us, then I lead Hal and the others. Hal knew where we should go, and what we should do. We were along for the ride.

---

[3] Thomas Merton, *Contemplation In a World of Action* (Notre Dame, Indiana: University of Notre Dame Press, 1998), p. 108.

[4] Adam Alter, *Irresistible: The Rise of Addictive Technology and the Business of Keeping Us Hooked* (New York: Penguin, 2017), pp. 107-109.

[5] Hal and Mirja Ronning head up the Institute for Bible Translators in Jerusalem. They also have taught at Hebrew University in Jerusalem.

At Redeemer, we believe God knows where we should go, and what we should do. God knows the universe's terrain better than I know the back of my hand. Thus, we are willing to be led by him. This is what we teach our people; viz., to listen to God's voice, and follow his leading.

The presence-driven leader is someone who is *led*. This is challenging in our American culture, where so many are addicted to being in control.[6] Being in control may sound safe, but it is a burden to need things to go your own way.

Thomas Merton writes:

> "I am tired of being my own Providence, of wanting and seeking things for myself, of making decisions for myself…, All I want, Jesus, is more and more to abandon everything to You. The more I go on, the more I realize I don't know where I am going. Lead me and take complete control of me."[7]

Presence-driven people, like Abraham, mostly (if not entirely) do not know where they are going. This is because they are *being led*, by God's Spirit. Oswald Chambers writes:

> "Have you ever "gone out" in this way? If so, there is no logical answer possible when anyone asks you what you are doing. One of the most difficult questions to answer in Christian work is, "What do you expect to do?" You don't know what you are going to do. The only thing you know is that God knows what He is doing."[8]

[6] On the idea of being addicted to control, see Gerald May, *Addiction and Grace* (New York: HarperOne, 2007).
[7] *A Year with Thomas Merton* (New York: HarperOne, 2004), June 23 entry.
[8] Oswald Chambers, *My Utmost for His Highest* (Grand Rapids: Discovery House, 1992).

Presence-driven leaders become like Peter, to whom Jesus said,

> *I'm telling you the very truth now: When you were young you dressed yourself and went wherever you wished, but when you get old you'll have to stretch out your hands while someone else dresses you and takes you where you don't want to go.*

And takes you where you don't want to go. This is hard for the control freak who, in their mind, is their own Providence. Presence-driven people trust God's leading. They understand the depth of their addiction to control, and their need to be released from the illusion that they are in control.[9]

Proverbs 3:5-6 counsels us to trust in the Lord, with a promise that he will direct our paths. To trust *is* to let go of control. So we pray, "God, lead us. Take us where you want us to go."

This is not a strategy. It is not a "ministry tool." It is a relationship. It is one thing: abide in God's presence. After that, it's the cloud during the day, and the pillar of fire by night. It is discerning, and obeying. It is following our Shepherd.

Presence-driven churches are low on strategizing, and high on abiding and obeying. So, at Redeemer we do not have a Five-Year Plan. Instead, we have a Now Plan. *Now* we will abide in Christ. *Now,* as he directs our paths, we will obey and follow.

Presence-driven people are the consummate followers. Merton expresses it this way.

> "The wonder of being brought, by God, around a corner and to realize a new road is opening up, perhaps—which He alone knows. And that there is no way of traveling it but in Christ and with Him. This is joy and peace—whatever

---

[9] This is similar to Jacques Ellul's "illusion of technique."

happens. The result does not matter. I have something to do for Him and, if I do that, everything else will follow."[10]

WE DISCERN, RATHER THAN DECIDE

At Redeemer, we don't "brainstorm." We don't "decide," as if our decisions affect God's plans and purposes for us. We *discern*, as best we can, what God is saying to us. Even if at times we discern wrongly, we are on board with the belief that discernment overrules decision-making.

I have attended, and even led, church meetings where we got together and "brainstormed," trying to figure out what we are to do. We stormed the gates of hell with our brains! Just us, assaulting darkness, using our collective cognitive abilities. I remember meetings where the walls were layered with ideas on paper, looking like Professor John Nash's garage in the movie "A Beautiful Mind."

I don't do this any longer. Not in our church. The presence-driven church is not a "brainstorming church." It is a discerning community. The difference between the two is vast.

Imagine the Apostle Paul at a brainstorming meeting. The ideas are pouring forth. The walls are coated with paper ideas. Paul, however, doesn't participate. Someone asks, "Why not?" Paul responds, "Why figure this out with our minds, since we have the mind of Christ?"[11]

The human mind is the craziest, most beautiful, impressive thing in the entire universe as we know it. It is complex, and mostly unfathomed. We are to love God with our minds. We are to think as well as we can. But the mind of Christ is more impressive. For one thing, God doesn't even need a brain to have a mind.[12]

---

[10] Thomas Merton, *A Year with Thomas Merton*, Kindle Locations 1209-1211.
[11] I Corinthians 2:16.
[12] God is a non-physical person.

God doesn't brainstorm. God has already-formulated ideas.[13] God is an all-knowing being, whose knowledge is vivid and immediate.[14] Our task is not to come up with more ideas, but to discern the mind of Christ and his vividly immediate thoughts.

I have found many pastors who agree with this. They have the sense that decision making in the church should look different than the corporate world. That difference is: God. God's presence. The biblical idea is that God is doing the leading. God is doing the building. Because unless God builds the house, we are thinking in vain.

What is needed is discernment. "Discernment," writes Barton, "in a most general sense, is the capacity to recognize and respond to the presence and the activity of God—both in the ordinary moments and in the larger decisions of our lives."[15]

Discernment is in direct proportion to familiarity. At Redeemer, we focus on familiarity with Jesus. Our ongoing transformation into Christlikeness, which happens in the presence of God and the Christ-abiding relationship, produces discernment. The more one knows Christ, with heart and mind, the more one becomes able to discern Christ. The apostle Paul says we are to be transformed by the renewing of our minds, so that we can discern what the will of God is; viz., that which is good, acceptable, and perfect.[16]

After hearing about the discernment-deciding distinction, a pastor at a conference in New York City confessed to me, "We never think this way. We just depend on our own thinking and planning and reasoning." And,

---

[13] Probably, God doesn't "formulate" anything, since an all-knowing being's knowledge would be immediate.

[14] Biblical references to God thinking, and pondering, are anthropomorphic. An all-knowing being would not have to figure things out. All knowledge would simply be there, vividly and immediately accessible. For an excellent source on this, see Wayne Grudem's *Systematic Theology* (Grand Rapids: Zondervan, 1994).

[15] Barton, *Pursuing God's Will Together: A Discernment Practice for Leadership Groups* (Downers Grove: InterVarsity, 2012), Kindle Locations 186-189.

[16] Romans 12:2.

he added, "If what you are saying is true, then my entire church will have to change!"

Correct. Presence-driven churches are transformed from decision-making to discerning the good and perfect will of God, which is a sign of our transformation.[17]

Presence-driven people soak in the rivers of ongoing renewal and transformation, in order to discern what the good and perfect will of God is. What else could spiritual leadership be, than to discern and do the will of God?

WE SHARE WHAT WE EXPERIENCE

Many churches encourage their people to share experiences and encounters with God. The same goes for us. Presence-driven churches share encounters with God, because being with God and knowing God by experience is the end-point of all creation.

Years ago, Jesus-rocker Larry Norman wrote a song called "Sweet Song of Salvation." The lyrics said, "When you know a pretty story, you don't let it go unsaid. You tell it to your children, before you tuck them into bed. And when you know a wonderful secret you tell it to your friends." I agree. Encounters with God cannot be contained. Leaders must provide an outlet for them to come forth.

When a fire is lit, it doesn't have to advertised or programmed. It does, however, need to be tended. One way we tend the fire is by sharing testimonies of God's presence. On a Sunday morning, for example, I will ask, "Has anyone had a God-encounter this past week, and, if so, would you be willing to share it, in a few sentences?" Always, there are some takers.

Long ago I discovered, when I am speaking, that not everyone is tuned in. I, like the apostle Paul, sadly report this to you. Actually, Paul had it worse,

---

[17] Ib.

since people died while he preached![18] But when our people step up to share their experiences with God, people lay their cell phones down, and lift their heads to listen. These testimonies are so encouraging! They build faith. They preach well.

Sharing our encounters with God throws more logs on the fire of his presence.

WE LEAN TOWARDS MINIMALISM

I pay a monthly fee to access and listen to every music cd that exists. I like multiple genres of music. One of them is minimalism. I listen to Steve Reich, Philip Glass, Brian Eno, Eric Satie, and their tribe.

I like minimalist repetition. I like the breathing room it gives me. Mostly, I do not care for over-production. I have a musical suspicion of over-production, tending to see it as a cover-up for poor musicianship.

The apostle Paul was a minimalist. As he traveled from church to church, across the first-century Roman Empire, he did not drag a production team with him. In I Corinthians 2:1-5, we see that Paul did not visit the Jesus-followers in Corinth with fog machines, black lights, powerful preaching, great intellectual arguments, stacks of Marshall amps, perfectly timed studio production quality music, a fair-trade coffee bar, tight jeans, stage lighting, creative videos, click tracks, and full color glossy programs. Instead, Paul came minimally, so that God might be worshiped maximally.

He writes:

> When I came to you, I did not come with eloquence or human wisdom
> as I proclaimed to you the testimony about God. For I resolved to know
> nothing while I was with you except Jesus Christ and him crucified. I

---

[18] Acts 20:9. "Seated in a window was a young man named Eutychus, who was sinking into a deep sleep as Paul talked on and on. When he was sound asleep, he fell to the ground from the third story and was picked up dead."

came to you in weakness with great fear and trembling. ⁴ My message and my preaching were not with wise and persuasive words, but with a demonstration of the Spirit's power, ⁵ so that your faith might not rest on human wisdom, but on God's power.

Paul arrived with two things:

1. Proclamation
2. Demonstration

Paul shared his testimony about God, and gave a demonstration of the Spirit's power. Nothing else. No crowd-pleasing techniques would be allowed to compete with Christ, and him crucified. Because if it turned into a production, people might rest their faith on the coffee, the jeans, and the fog, rather than on God's power.

At Redeemer, we are not "putting on our best" for visitors. We are clearing away obstacles, so God can display his best. We believe God brings his best wherever two or more are gathered. If God leads you to bring out the special drama, the kids choir, and the pancake breakfast (with maple syrup), then do it, out of obedience. Otherwise, God's earth-shattering presence is more than enough, better than the pancakes.[19]

On Sunday mornings we prepare to worship, preach, and pray. This is our minimalist structure, within which God's presence has space and time to move. For example, this past Easter Sunday I preached about knowing Christ and the power of his resurrection. Then, we prayed for sick people who were there. As far as I could tell, the man who came with his hip out of socket, causing him a lot of pain, experienced healing. Someone told me afterward, "Did you see the smile on his face as the pain had left him? Did you see him walking afterward carrying his cane but not using it?" This past weekend, weeks after Easter, there he was, walking normally and without pain. Within the minimalist structure, the maximalist God moves.

---

[19] Let me be clear. If God says, "Have a pancake breakfast," then obey and do it. To the best of your ability. And, expect God to be there.

We worship. We experience God. The gifts of the Spirit are manifested. God demonstrates his power. Everyone gets to participate. Every Sunday is Easter. Beyond that, what more could there be?

I've had many beautiful, touching worship experiences in my life. Sometimes it's happened when I've been alone, sometimes with a small group of people, and sometimes in large group settings. When the real worship thing happens, it is 100% about God and his presence. For me, this *never* has to do with how good the worship musicians are, or even if there are worship musicians.

For example, I was preaching in Kurnool, in central India, in an old church building on the Deccan plateau, before a thousand people. There was no worship band. I am not against worship bands. It's just that they are unnecessary for worship to happen. In this falling-apart church building, one man was leading the people in a worship song, *a capella*. It was in the Telegu dialect. The singing was repetitive, and went on for a long time. In the middle of it, *it happened*. God! In my heart, I was loving and adoring him. I was caught up in God's presence, 100%.

David Platt writes:

> "What if we take away the cool music and the cushioned chairs? What if the screens are gone and the stage is no longer decorated? What if the air conditioning is off and the comforts are removed? Would His Word still be enough for his people to come together?"[20]

In some churches, it might not be. When all is stripped away, few would simply come. For the people in my church, perhaps like yours, God's presence is not only enough, it is our reason for meeting.

---

[20] David Platt, *Radical: Taking Back Your Faith from the American Dream* (Colorado Springs: Multnomah, 2010), p. 27.

WE NURTURE OUR DISTINCTIVENESS

Most of the students in my college philosophy classes are unimpressed by, and uninterested in, "relevant" churches; viz., entertainment churches that cater to our consumer culture. The consumer-driven strategy, I observe, is not working. There may be entertainment churches that are large in size, but if what they have gathered is an audience, it is not a movement.

For the Jesus Movement to go forward, we must not make it our goal to "blend in."[21] The danger of blending in with our secular culture is that, in the process, the culture will colonize us. Instead, we choose to lock into our distinctives, and go with them.

What, then, is our distinctive? The presence-driven church's great distinctive is: *We have God, and God's presence.* We have answers to ultimate questions. We have Christ in us, the hope of glory. That's not bad. And, by the way, the core distinctives cost no money to maintain.[22]

In a quote that has greatly influenced me, Yale theologian Miroslav Volf writes:

> "Christian communities will be able to survive and thrive in contemporary societies only if they attend to their "difference" from surrounding cultures and subcultures. The following principle stands: *whoever wants the Christian communities to exist must want their difference from the surrounding culture, not their blending into it.* As a consequence, Christian communities must "manage" their identity by actively engaging in "boundary maintenance." Without boundaries, communities dissolve."[23]

---

[21] See Os Guinness, *Prophetic Untimeliness: A Challenge to the Idol of Relevance* (Grand Rapids: Baker, 2003).

[22] The first church, in the book of Acts, didn't have a building, therefore they didn't have a budget.

[23] Miroslav Volf, *A Public Faith* (Grand Rapids: Brazos, 2013), p. 81. Emphasis mine.

Eugene Peterson consistently says the same thing. He writes, "The church in which I live and have been called to write and speak has become more like the culture... than counter to it."[24]

When God's presence is not the focus of Church, when the Church thing is not 100% about God, when the emphasis is on controlling things and people and "the program," when *chronos* prevails over *kairos*, when pressure mounts to keep people coming and add more people to maintain the growing infrastructure, the dust of death rises from the absence of God.[25]

James McDonald writes:

> "Whether you are 15 people around a coffee table or 150 people in a tired building trying to turn it around or 1,500 people on the rise with plans for another service – regardless of size: if you don't have the thing that makes us distinct, you have nothing, no matter what you have. And if you do have it – what we were made to long for; what makes us a true church of the one true God – you have everything you need, no matter what you lack."[26]

Great leaders point us to our distinctives. E. Stanley Jones was a missionary to India. He spoke to Gandhi once, and asked him, "How can we make Christianity naturalized in India?" Gandhi's response included this nugget of wisdom. He replied, "Practice your religion with adulterating it or toning it down."[27]

---

[24] Eugene Peterson, *Living the Resurrection: The Risen Christ in Everyday Life* (Colorado Springs: NavPress, 2014), Kindle Locations 107-108.

[25] In *The Dust of Death* (Wheaton: Crossway, 1994), Os Guinness showed how the counterculture (which has now become the culture) fails to provide an effective alternative to faith.

[26] James McDonald, *Vertical Church*, Kindle Locations 1003-1006.

[27] In R. L. Deats, *Mahatma Gandhi: Non-Violent Liberator; A Biography* (Hyde Park, NY: New City Press, 1951), p. 39.

At Redeemer, we focus on the presence of God, and its implications. This emphasis has made us sufficiently *different* from the surrounding culture. We are so different that some, even other Christians, label us as the "weird" church. If "weird" means "makes way for God's presence," then I gladly live with that. Even more, we desire that. We pursue that.

How crucial is this, in such times as we are now in? Rod Dreher writes:

> "I have written *The Benedict Option* to wake up the church and to encourage it to act to strengthen itself, while there is still time. If we want to survive, we have to return to the roots of our faith, both in thought and in practice. We are going to have to learn habits of the heart forgotten by believers in the West. We are going to have to change our lives, and our approach to life, in radical ways. In short, *we are going to have to be the church*, without compromise, no matter what it costs."[28]

WE DON'T STRIVE TO MAKE THINGS HAPPEN

At Redeemer, we have a "No Striving" rule. We do not try to make things happen. That's when things get stagy. We don't focus on trying to "get things going." Our belief is that God will lead us to what we are, and are not, to do.

We teach our people to abide in Christ, like a branch connected to a vine. Then, we rest on the promise that, as Jesus said, our lives will bear much fruit.

When God directs, then we work hard. But we are not first working hard, and afterwards baptizing our efforts in prayer.

---

[28] Rod Dreher, *The Benedict Option: A Strategy for Christians in a Post-Christian Nation* (New York: Penguin, 2017), pp. 3-4.

WE DON'T CONTROL PEOPLE

I admire the writings of Keith Miller. Years ago, Linda and I read *The Taste of New Wine* and loved it. Later, I read Keith's *A Hunger for Healing*, which was a killer book for me. More recently, I picked up his book *Compelled to Control*.

In a presence-driven church the leaders are not compelled to control. When God is in control there is no need to control people. And, it is foolish to think we can control God. I cannot predict what God is going to do. God's knowledge and ways are infinitely beyond mine. So, I must let go of the need to know everything. This is not easy, but it is the Big One when it comes to Normal Church. This is exemplified in the old saying, "Let go, and let God." This requires letting go of our own agendas and our need to control things. For pastors, it means giving Sunday mornings over to God.

Many people, including Christians, are control freaks. The people they control are controlees. Linda and I see marriages that are the coming together of these two types. Every control freak needs a controlee, and vice versa. There are a lot of "master/slave" marriages out there. There are also plenty of master/slave churches.

I think we all struggle with the control thing. Control is the antithesis of trust. Trust is huge in the Jesus-life, and life in general, since we control so very, very little. Miller writes: "control is the major factor in destroying intimate relationships."[29]

Why do we do this? Why do we try to control others, even while we can't control our own selves, being ourselves out of control? Miller writes:

> "The fear of being revealed as a failure, as not being "enough" somehow, is a primary feeling that leads to the compulsion to control other people. When we were children, the fear of being inadequate and shameful was

---

[29] J. Keith Miller, *Compelled to Control* (Deerfield Beach, Florida: Health Communications, 1997), p. 7.

tied to our terror of being deserted or rejected and we had little control over getting what we needed. To counteract that basic terror, we have evidently been trying all our lives in various ways to "get control" of life. This includes controlling other people."[30]

A controlling person is un-free. I like the way Richard Foster once put this: God wants to free us from the terrible burden of always having to get our own way. "Walking in freedom" and "controlling other people" ("always getting our own way") are antithetical.

I'm praying to be less controlling, and more trusting in God when it comes to other people. Note: this is about trusting God even when you don't trust other people. To trust God when around distrustful people *is* an experiential act of freedom.

This is what the presence of God brings to us. God tells us we are not inadequate and shameful. The more of God's experienced presence there is in a community, the less control there is. We truly can let God, and let go. We substitute control for trust. God's presence creates a trusting environment. In his presence, we feel safe.

My church, the people I fellowship with and love dearly, is not a perfect place. The atmosphere is not always control-free. But we do talk and teach about not micromanaging others. Our core leaders exemplify this. You would have to visit and talk with our people to know this. My people do not feel their pastor is trying to control them.[31]

Precisely because we teach that everyone is called to abide in Christ, that everyone has access to God's kingdom, it follows that everyone can discern and hear the voice of God. Everyone can be led by God's Spirit. When my brother or sister is led by God, it will always look different from how I would do it. This realization frees me from controlling others.

---

[30] Ib., p. 14
[31] If this is not true, then I am a blind man in trouble.

This means that *everyone in a presence-driven church is a leader.*

WE SEE PEOPLE BECOMING LEADERS

One of our young men, a former atheist, came to me after a Sunday morning God event. Jesse told me he was praying, and heard God speak to him. "I felt," he said, "God tell me I was to have a showing of the movie "God's Not Dead" at Redeemer. And that you were to have a Q&A afterwards."

I replied, "I agree. And, Jesse, you are the leader."

Jesse said, "Really?"

Yes, really. No bureaucratic hoops to jump through. No committee meetings, no congregational voting.

Jesse and I met three times in preparation for the event. He had never done this before. He formed a team to assist him. He purchased the viewing rights to the movie. I helped him with the process. At one point Jesse said, "This is the greatest thing I have ever done in my life."

Two hundred showed up for the movie. When the movie was about to begin, I went to the sound booth where Jesse was. I told him, "Look at the people, Jesse. Look what God is doing through you!" He looked, and said nothing. Jesse is a leader.

In the presence-driven church, every follower of Jesus has intimate access to God's presence. As we teach our people to abide in Christ, the environment becomes organic. Fruit-bearing happens. The presence-driven church not only sanctions this, but demands it. "Church" becomes a place where, as John Wimber once said, "everyone gets to play."

My church has become a place where all our people can fulfill their God-given visions and dreams. This is because, in the presence-driven church, we don't have pastors channeling people into what the pastor does and doesn't want, with the pastor then striving and sweating to recruit people to a vision the people don't have a heart for.

I expect God to speak to my people. God gives them visions of how to follow and serve him. When this happens, the visionary recipient becomes the leader, with me as their pastor, championing their leadership. One benefit is I don't have to hype the vision. Nor do I have to recruit for it. It just happens, as led by God's empowering presence. This deeply affects me. I have changed, in many ways, in this kind of culture. This was how I became a pastor.

My transition from spectator to leader came through a church bulletin announcement. It altered the course of my life forever. I was twenty-one, and a brand new Jesus-follower. My heart was untainted by church politics (or any politics). My knowledge of the Bible was slim. I just knew I had been rescued by Jesus, and loved him for this.

The line in the bulletin read: "Please pray that our church would find a new youth leader." This was Tabor Lutheran Church, in Rockford, Illinois. I grew up in Tabor. I liked my church family. My father served as a deacon. He was a quiet man, so it still creates wonder in me to think that he taught Sunday School, and I was in one of his classes.

I was never involved in Tabor's youth group, being consumed with playing sports and practicing guitar. I never led anything like a Sunday School class or a Bible study, nor would have wanted to. I'd never prayed out loud. I rarely prayed at all. I didn't turn to God for anything, ever, until the day when, in my desperation, I said, "God, if you are real, help me." Which he did.

For two Sundays in a row, the line in the bulletin read, "Please pray that our church would find a new youth leader." You mean we haven't found one yet? The kids in this church need a leader! Having been spiritually leaderless myself, I knew this to be fact. Every kid needs a mentor. I had been mentored by my secular peers, did a lot of self-mentoring, and the results were disastrous. I was "lost." But now, at last, was "found." I wanted Tabor's teens to experience The Rescue, as I had.

On week three of the announcement I came to Sunday morning worship service looking forward to, of all things, reading the bulletin. There it was: "Please pray that our church would find a new youth leader." I felt an urgency about this. I began praying. Throughout the following week this was on my prayer list: "O God, please, please bring someone to help our church's youth!" And then it happened. I told God, sounding like Abraham's wife Sarah, "Surely you are joking?"

I called Pastor Harvey Johnson and made an appointment to get together. I had never done anything like this before. (The words "I've never done anything like this before" were to become thematic in my life.) I wonder what he thought I wanted to talk about?

I admired and respected Pastor Johnson. I was nervous the day I met with him. Part of me felt foolish, a rookie with zero job experience, applying for a position that begged for credentials.

"I have seen the announcement in the bulletin. Has any progress been made on finding a youth leader?"

No.

I can't remember the exact words I used next. Somehow, I expressed my idea, my sense, that God was appealing to me to work as Tabor's Youth Leader. I remember feeling how unwise this sounded to me. I told Pastor Johnson about my new life in Christ, and confessed I had not even heard the words "seminary training" before. After much listening and sharing, he affirmed my calling. "I think God wants you to do this, so let's do it." He seemed genuinely grateful that God had finally answered his prayers.

Sometimes I have wondered what my life would look like had that announcement not been in the bulletin, or if Tabor found another youth leader, or if Pastor Johnson had told me, "John, you don't have the training and experience for this." That would have been understandable. I am still amazed that he supported me in this!

There was more to come. One day, while praying, I felt God calling me to preach a sermon, on a Sunday morning, in my church. I had never done this before! Not only that, I was afraid to speak in front of groups.

I went to Pastor Johnson and shared this with him. To my amazement, he agreed that God was leading me to do this. So, on a Sunday morning at Tabor Lutheran Church in Rockford, Illinois, I preached a sermon in front of hundreds of people, to include my parents. I remain thankful to Pastor Harvey Johnson for allowing me to do this. It was life-giving to my spiritual formation, and part of my calling to be a pastor.

In the presence-driven church the people know that *they are the church, and that God can lead them* to do great things to advance his kingdom. This strengthens the community, and develops us all into leaders. I love standing back and seeing God lead my brothers and sisters do great things for Christ!

We are becoming a community of leaders, where the people are converted to community. Just last week, for example, I declared over my church that we are all ambassadors for Christ. Then, I pointed out several people by name, saying "There is Ambassador Pat, and over there is Ambassador Jaime, and Ambassador Paul," and so on.

In a presence-driven church the people get called. We champion this, and allow people to follow God's leading. This changes us forever. Like Moses, when he received a call from God. Ruth Haley Barton writes:

> "When God spoke to him out of the burning bush, he was asking Moses to take the difficult journey of "rising to personality"—rising to the full purpose of his being here on earth—in order to realize the meaning of his life. He

was asking him to become more fully the person he had always been and at the same time to transcend it."[32]

Few things are more beautiful to me than seeing people emerge out of the passive, cocooned audience and grow the wings of leadership. Such was my calling to be a pastor. I began to shepherd Tabor's teens. In a few months Linda would join me. Now I see God's hand in it all, and have *never* wanted to rewind my life so things would turn out differently.

AUTHENTIC COMMUNITY EMERGES OUT OF GOD'S PRESENCE

Every week, for over forty years, I have gone to lonely places and prayed for three to six hours.[33] One fruit of my praying life is that I grow in compassion and love for others. Had I not engaged in the praying life, my progress in love would have atrophied. A disconnected branch produces no fruit. This ravages and decimates authentic community.

We teach our people how to pray in solitude. Then, we see how solitary praying transforms our heart into a heart for others. A heart for others compels one to engage in community. Without a heart for others, community relationships degenerate into individualism and competition.

Spiritual formation always leads to formation to life, in community. We cannot consistently dwell in God's presence and resist community. When God shows up, it's for *us*, collectively.

The spiritual movement is like this: Journey inward, journey outward; journey alone, journey together. Solitary praying is the foundation for authentic community. And then,

> "The more genuine and the deeper our community becomes, the more will everything else between us recede, the more clearly and purely will Jesus Christ and his work

---

[32] Barton, *Strengthening the Soul of Your Leadership*, p. 83.

[33] My book *Praying* is a record of this.

become the one and only thing that is vital between us. We have one another only through Christ, but through Christ we do have one another, wholly, and for all eternity."[34]

In the transforming community, the abiding life comes first. The life and love that form true fellowship can only be found in the presence of the One who is Life and Love. This happens from the inside out.

WE FIND HEALING IN HIS PRESENCE

The presence-driven church has a healing environment. This is because God is in the house, with all his essential attributes. When God presences among us we are with an all-knowing, all-powerful, all-loving Being. We are with a perfect agent of redemption. We encounter the presence of the Lord, who is our healer.[35]

I performed the funeral services for my mother and father, and Linda's mother and father. Linda's dad lived with us for seven years. He passed away at 2:06 am, on New Year's Eve day, 2012. That night we got two hours of sleep.

As the day went on, we knew we wanted to spend the night with our church family. Many were gathering at the church building at 9 PM to worship and pray in the new year. Linda and I needed to be in God's empowering presence, and our presence-filled community. What a beautiful, healing night that was for us.

The reality of God's presence is not, for us, a religious theory. It is a visceral, existential, felt-reality. We desire it, and wonder where we would be without it. To live out of the presence of God is to exist outside the walls of God's omni-protective fortress. Linda and I know God as our fortress and strength, an ever-present help in trouble. To live apart from God is to be troubled. We found, on that New Year's Eve, healing for our troubledness.

---

[34] Dietrich Bonhoeffer, cited in Ib., p. 86.
[35] "I am the LORD, your healer." Exodus 15:26.

I love how Henri Nouwen expresses this as he writes:

> "Once I "know" God, that is, once I experience God's love
> as the love in which all my experiences are anchored, I can
> desire only one thing: to be in that love. "Being" anywhere
> else, then, is shown to be illusory and eventually lethal."[36]

When we gather together we expect healing and deliverance to take place. I saw this happen on a Sunday morning in the spring of 2017. One of our friends, Sherry, has had chronic back problems for a long time. This causes her great pain, so much so that she barely can get down the basement stairs of her house. On that morning, I heard God say to me, "Call Sherry forward, and pray for her."

Sherry is open to receiving healing prayers. She and her husband Dave have been with Redeemer longer than I have. Many know her back issues, and pray for her.

I called Sherry forward. I placed my hand on her shoulder[37], and said, "Thank you, God, for healing power." I want my people to remember that the power to heal is from God, not a mere human like me.

I then said, "In Jesus' name, be healed."

After waiting a moment, I asked Sherry, "Do you sense God doing anything in you?" She replied, "I feel tingling in my body."

"God is doing something, Sherry. May I pray again?"

I did. And Sherry, before her many friends, bent down and touched her hands to the ground, feeling no pain. She stood tall, and did a little dance in a circle. Our people applauded and rejoiced. Faith and expectation increased. God's presence felt weighty and thick. In that atmosphere, I invited any who

---

[36] Henri Nouwen, *The Only Necessary Thing* (New York: Crossroad, 2008), p. 69

[37] Candy Gunther Brown calls this "PIP," proximal intercessory prayer. See Brown, *Testing Prayer: Science and Healing* (Cambridge, MA: Harvard University Press, 2012).

would like healing prayers to raise their hands. Several did. I then asked our people to surround them, and pray for them. Many did.

One of our healing stories was published in Craig Keener's book *Miracles: The Credibility of the New Testament Accounts*.[38] We have experienced several people being healed, to the present moment. Our people have discovered that, where God is, there is power and love.

WE EXPECT AND EMBRACE CHANGE

I was told of a speaker who came to Redeemer before I was there. He talked about the need to welcome change. Yes, change is hard. But a presence-driven church will experience constant change, so you must get used to it. He said, "You should change at least one thing in this sanctuary every week. Even if it is simply to hang the banner on the left wall on the right wall." Slowly, over the years, I see that many of our people have gotten over the fear of change. But it still can be hard.

Linda and I had planned to be in Green Lake, Wisconsin, as our annual HSRM conference was to begin the next day.[39] We were all packed, ready and excited to go. But we did not. Linda's father Del's defibrillator went off, twice.

We took Del to the ICU at St. Vincent's Hospital in Toledo. I will never forget that ride, praying Del would not die before we got there. Our plans had changed. Del's plans changed. But God had plans. We were to align with what God was doing.

It is a horrible thing to hear someone scream when their defibrillator goes off. It is more horrible for that person. Decisions must be made - to go to the ER, or not? It's not always clear. For the caregiver, the unclarity is hard.

---

[38] Keener, *Miracles: The Credibility of the New Testament Accounts* (Baker: Grand Rapids, 2011). See Vol. I, p. 440.

[39] I am blessed to be Co-Director of Holy Spirit Renewal Ministries; hsrm.org.

We don't always know if we are making the right decisions. And, sometimes, there's no time to sit back and weigh alternatives.

For Linda and me, the voice of God was clear: we were to stay with Del. He felt he had interrupted our plans. But, of course, that was not true. As Linda told him, "Dad, you would do the same thing for us."

It's normal to feel disappointed when you're all packed, ready to go, and the interruption comes. Henri Nouwen once complained to God about this, and God told him "these interruptions are your life."

Life is not about "us," and "our plans." It's at points like these that we see what kind of spiritual life we have. Life *is* a series of interruptions. Within this life, the Holy Spirit interrupts, in his typical non-programmatic and unpredictable way. How we respond is crucial, both to what God is doing, and to the formation of Christ in us.

How grateful I am that my church community is interruptible. When God changes direction, and I share this with my people, there are often cheers and applause. We are in a place where we expect to be interrupted by God. To go on uninterrupted is a sign that something is wrong.

Perhaps your church family thinks this way. If so, it is beautiful. At Redeemer, being interruptible in response to change directly affects our worship experience.

GOD LEADS US AS WE WORSHIP

We cannot program or predict how the Holy Spirit will lead. I assume you agree with me, right? We do not have epistemic access to the all-knowing mind of the Spirit. This is true for all of life, including what happens on Sunday mornings.

When Sunday morning arrives, we do have some things in place: an opening worship song, we call our children to the altar and pray for them, announcements (if any), praise & worship, preaching, then a time of ministry. But all this can, and does, change. Every Sunday morning.

It happened last week. I was on the platform with our worship team, when a girl named Avery was brought forward by her mother, Melissa. Avery has a neurological condition that prevents her from exercising normal cognitive and physical functions. She loves worship music, especially the guitars. Melissa brings her to the altar steps. Avery sits on the floor and moves with the music.

As Avery was worshiping, one of our men came forward and began praying for her. Then, one by one, more people came. Some knelt next to her. A host of people surrounded Avery, praying for her. It was beautiful and powerful! And unprogrammed. At times like this I often think, "Here at Redeemer we are not on *chronos* time, but *kairos* time." A presence-driven church is not bound by the clock, or the bulletin.

We begin with a simple, basic structure. That's OK and, I think, good. But within this structure, there is room for the Spirit to do his thing. And he does. Always, in our context.

In that sense, we do not have a preset order of events. While God can, and does, pre-order what happens in our corporate gatherings, it is *God*, not I or a committee, doing the pre-ordering. We cannot order or program God.

I appreciate theologian John Jefferson Davis's focus on the presence motif in his book *Worship and the Reality of God: An Evangelical Theology of Real Presence.* To experience God in our midst as we gather together - that is our reason for being.

Davis summarizes his thoughts:

> "Because the living God, the risen Christ and the Holy Spirit are present in the midst of the assembly, true worship takes place in kingdom space and kingdom time, where ordinary space and time are altered by the massive reality of

the Creator and Redeemer of space and time, where earth is lifted up to heaven, and the future impinges on the present. The meeting space is spiritually energized and charged by the presence of the Spirit, the Shekinah Glory; ordinary time is suffused with the power of the past redemptive events of the incarnation, cross and resurrection, and anticipates the revelation of the Christ who is to come and who will usher in the new creation."[40]

When God shows up in our worship, space and time pause.[41] Things are different. The ordinary becomes the extraordinary, the natural becomes the supernatural, the secular transforms into the spiritual, the mundane gets energized by the powerful presence of God. And we are swept along, as the Spirit leads us further up and further in to God's weighty presence.

WE AFFIRM FEELINGS AND EMOTIONS

"When I entered your church's sanctuary I felt the presence of God."

Over my twenty-five years at Redeemer I have heard these words often, in many variations, spoken by people new to our Jesus-community.

"I sensed God's peace as I approached your building."

"I encountered God's power as I worshiped with your people."

"Surely the Lord is in this place."

I experience this, too. This is how things should be when the church gathers. Jesus-followers encounter, regularly, the earth-shattering presence of God. My church family attests to this as commonplace.

---

[40] Davis, *Worship and the Reality of God*, Kindle Locations 992-993.

[41] I am using a metaphor to describe a *kairos* experience. For some heavy hitting on the subject of time and the word "now," see physicist Richard Muller, *Now: The Physics of Time* (New York: W.W. Norton, 2016). My metaphor will no longer seem so figurative.

Presence-drivenness is not about a physical building, but a people who host the presence of God. Remember how Jesus changed the whole Temple concept from a physical structure to a people, individually (I Cor. 3:16), and corporately (I Cor. 6:19). In the first verse, the word 'you' is singular; in the second verse, the word 'you' is plural. God comes to dwell among his people, to inhabit his lovers, in their singular hearts, and in their plural midst. We become portable sanctuaries. This is a visceral, experiential reality. One *feels* God, within and without.

As God lavishly pours his love into our hearts, this is best understood as a feeling. My Jewish wife Linda understands this, since Hebrew spirituality is full-bodied.[42] My evangelical heritage pauses at this point, warning me about the dangers of "feelings." I tended to value the dispassionate "Mr. Spock" over the emotional "Kirk."[43] But surely all talk about God's love is meaning-deficient if it does not include feeling. Spock and Kirk are both needed to pilot the Enterprise on its mission.

Consider these words from Robert Barclay, written in 1701.

> "When I came into the silent assemblies of God's people,
> I felt a secret power among them, which touched my heart.
> And as I gave way to it, I found the evil in me weakening,
> and the good lifted up. Thus it was that I was knit into
> them and united with them. And I hungered more and
> more for the increase of this power and life until I could
> feel myself perfectly redeemed."[44]

When we speak of God's presence, we do so in the language of emotions and feelings. When two or more are gathered, he is with us, and not just intellectually. Emotions and feelings are, as the philosopher Ludwig

---

[42] Linda's mother Martha was Jewish. Martha became a follower of Jesus, and her husband Del and daughters Vicki, Linda, and Lora followed.

[43] The main characters on the original Star Trek television series. My Finnish background predisposed me to unemotionalism.

[44] Cited in Richard Foster, *Sanctuary of the Soul: Journey into Meditative Prayer* (Downers Grove: InterVarsity, 2011), Kindle Locations 302-304.

Wittgenstein might say, the "language game" of God's presence. *Feeling* is essential in *knowing* God.

At Redeemer, we value emotions and feelings. We don't stir them up and manipulate people. (I dread this happening!) But when our people feel God-with-them, we cry "he touched me," deep within, in our hearts, as the joy of the Lord fills our souls.

OUR PRIMARY FOCUS IS NOT ON MEETING PEOPLE'S NEEDS

Our primary focus, our distinctive, is God and his presence. Other things, while important, are secondary. Such as, meeting people's needs.

We believe the greatest need humanity has *is* the Lord.

I recall the Steve Green song "People Need the Lord." It moved me. I affirmed the theology behind it, and felt God's presence as I worshiped by it. Are my deepest needs met in God's presence? Yes. Because what I primordially need is God.

Some churches focus on meeting the individual needs of people as their *raison d-etre*, their way of life. Everything gets oriented towards this. This is a mistake, and makes solving conflict more difficult. James van Yperen writes:

> "In many churches, the remedy for conflict often makes it worse, deepening the problem by failing to address the fundamental issue: We are trusting our ways more than God's. All individualism leads to consumerism. When self is center, the world exists to meet one's personal needs. "Hey, I'm entitled to this!" A culture of consumerism will always value individual needs above community life. "You're important to me so long as you serve my needs." When a church focuses on meeting the needs of individuals, Jesus and the Bible become a personal, need-meeting machine. The church becomes a collection of

individuals who are fundamentally at competition with one another—competing to have their needs met. Here, the Gospel becomes a commodity distributed by supply and demand. Since no church can meet all the needs, ultimately one set of needs must be placed against the other. When this happens, staff and members will compete to make a case for how and why their needs are greater than others.... [T]he church becomes divided into interest groups or coalitions formed by age and individual preference."[45]

A presence-driven church is not a shopping center where we pick and choose what is good for us. Instead, the overwhelming, primary focus is God. God comes before us. God, before me. I decrease, so that he might increase. All my deepest needs are met in Christ.

There are, of course, countless benefits of abiding in God's presence. Sometimes we show up begging on Sunday morning. My people have been taught that the solution is intimate contact and connection with God. Our American culture is clueless about such things. But in my church, we have not forgotten his benefits.

At Redeemer, we believe everything is available in God's presence. So, we teach people how to access the presence of God. This, said Dallas Willard, is the "gospel"; i.e., the good news that followers of Jesus have access to the kingdom of God.[46]

WE DON'T SPEND MONEY ON ADVERTISING

We don't need to promote God, right? If it's really *God* that shows up and inhabits the house, the word will get around just fine without advertising.

---

[45] James van Yperen, *Making Peace: A Guide to Overcoming Church Conflict* (Chicago: Moody, 2002), p. 30.

[46] In Dallas Willard and Gary Moon, *Eternal Living: Reflections on Dallas Willard's Teaching on Faith and Formation* (Downers Grove: InterVarsity, 2015), Kindle Location 2263.

People will ask, "How was church today?" You will answer, "God made an appearance."

Focus on God's presence, and your church's advertising budget may flatline. If God leads you to spend money on advertising, then obey! As for us, we have found that the presence of God advertises itself.

Anyway, some advertising is just hype, right? I witnessed this when, years ago, a church paid for a large ad in one of our area newspapers. The ad called this church "The Friendliest Church in America." When I read that, I immediately thought, "We're #2!" In a few years that church imploded, and the pastor left. The friendliest church in America was filled with conflict.

A.W. Tozer writes:

> "Every age has its own characteristics. Right now we are in an age of religious complexity. The simplicity which is in Christ is rarely found among us. In its stead are programs, methods, organizations and a world of nervous activities which occupy time and attention but can never satisfy the longing of the heart. The shallowness of our inner experience, the hollowness of our worship, and the servile imitation of the world which marks our promotional methods all testify that we, in this day, know God only imperfectly, and the peace of God scarcely at all. If we would find God amid all the religious externals we must first determine to find Him."[47]

WE PRIVILEGE *AISTHESIS* BEFORE *NOESIS*

Many of us who are theologians are following the career of James K. A. Smith. The oddity of Smith is that he is Pentecostal, a brilliant philosopher, and a professor at Calvin College. Think about this. My initial attraction

---

[47] A. W. Tozer, *The Pursuit of God*, Kindle Locations 128-133.

to him was that I am Pentecostal, a philosopher (not as brilliant), and teach philosophy at our local community college.[48]

So, I bought one of his books. How could I resist the title *Thinking in Tongues: Pentecostal Contributions to Christian Philosophy*? In this book Pentecostalism combines with logic. Smith has much to say on the logic and heart of worship. He writes:

> "Pentecostal worship operates on the tacit assumption that we are moved by stories.[49]

> [F]ilm operates on the same assumption - as does literature. One could see, then, how the affectivity of pentecostal spirituality resonates with the imaginative arts.[50]

> Indeed, I would suggest that a pentecostal epistemology is always already a kind of *aesthetic*, an epistemic grammar that privileges *aesthesis* (experience) before *noesis* (intellection)...

> Pentecostalism is marked, even defined, by an openness to "signs and wonders"; as such, it is a spirituality of signs, of the visible and the invisible - it is a religion of manifesting, displaying, and showing. Pentecostal spirituality and worship are very much a visual economy, a spectacular, visible, fantastic world of the sort created by the fantastic world of film. Like the visual world of film, pentecostal

---

[48] Lest you be frightened, the answer is "No. Your church does not have to be Pentecostal to be presence-driven." Still, I find Pentecostalism friendlier towards experience, emotion, and feeling as ways of knowing, than is classical Evangelical theology (my background.).

[49] Smith, *Thinking in* Tongues, p. 82. Of course we are moved by stories, more than by theories. Hence, movies. Compare N.T. Wright's narrative theology. And, note the place of "testimony" in Pentecostalism, which Smith calls "the poetry of Pentecostal experience." (Kindle Location 279)

[50] See, for example, my church's sanctuary, which is bursting with original art created by our people.

worship is semiotic[51]; but also like film, it is more than visual, affecting other senses and affecting us via narrative, etc."

At a recent Elders meeting one of our leaders commented on what we see happening on Sunday mornings. He said, "I feel like we're in Narnia!" We are, as N.T. Wright has taught us, participants in the fifth act of the five-act Grand Narrative of Scripture; which is, "the New Testament and the People of God."[52]

My academic training is overwhelmingly in *noesis*, while looking with a crooked eye towards *aesthesis*. But slowly, over time, I've left my near-total *noesis* paradigm and embraced *aesthesis*.

A presence-driven church will value both, with *aesthesis* being our final destination.

WE HAVE LEFT OUR COMFORT ZONES BEHIND

By nature, presence-driven churches have abandoned the idea of "comfort zones." I have found that, whenever Christ leads me, it is out of my comfort zone. I assume God sympathizes with our weakness, while not being coerced by it.

You can forget all talk of "comfort zones" and "bucket lists." Abram did not know where he was going. Neither do I. God's destination was not on Abraham's bucket list. Many in my church understand and accept this. When God leads, they follow.

We risk all on the following: *It is possible to hear God, and be led by God.* If God does not speak, we will not act but wait (no activity for activity's sake; no panic-room, knee-jerk "doing"). When God leads, we will obey. As for

---

[51] Semiotics is the science of signs/signifiers.
[52] See N. T. Wright, *The New Testament and the People of God* (Philadelphia: Fortress, 1992), and *Scripture and the Authority of God: How to Read the Bible Today* (New York: HarperOne, 2013).

our destination, we don't know, except that it will be good, and bring glory to God.

In this chapter I have shared some things I know about my church, as one example of a presence-driven church. Hopefully, this has given you some ideas of what to expect, and what to look for.

I want to say, again, that my church is not without problems and imperfections. We, and I, do not always hear correctly. Still, there are essentials of the presence-driven church, as well as non-essentials that apply to individual churches. My church and your church will be the same genus, but different species. Therefore, there is no formula for developing presence-driven churches. That the Holy Spirit is allowed, and expected, to lead, is common to all. How the Spirit leads will result in our differences.

LEADERSHIP APPLICATION

Being Presence-Driven means something, and looks like something. I suggest pastors and leaders help their people by:

1) Pointing out and explaining core elements of a presence-driven church, as seen in your church.
2) Discerning, and sharing, specific leadings of the Holy Spirit in your church family.
3) Being prepared to be led by God and "interrupt" whatever plans you may have on Sunday morning. Pastors — as you are worshiping, if God leads you to share something while the worship is going on, step up to the microphone, alert your worship leader to lower the volume, and speak to your people something like this: "As we were worshiping, I felt God leading us to pause and pray for _____ who is going through a difficult time."
4) Doing a book study using the best book on discernment, which is: *Pursuing God's Will Together: A Discernment Practice for Leadership Groups.*[53]

---

[53] Another excellent book is Henri Nouwen, *Discernment: Reading the signs of Daily Life* (New York: HarperOne, 2015).

7

THE LANGUAGE OF THE PRESENCE-DRIVEN CHURCH

In this chapter I make the following claim: *Presence-driven churches speak a unique language. This is important, because language constitutes our experience of reality, to include the experience of God's presence.* This claim is informed by my doctoral work in linguistics, philosophy of language, and metaphor theory. I'll begin with a story.

I was flying from Detroit to Nairobi, Kenya, to preach in a church, and lead a conference for pastors from Kenya and Uganda. I like to read as much as I can about the culture I'm going to, so I brought a few books for the long flight.

One was *Decolonizing the Mind*, by radical Kenyan writer Ngugi Wa Thiong'o. Wa Thiong'o's challenge to African peoples is to abandon the languages of the culture that colonized them, and return to full adoption of their native dialects. This is because *in a language there is an embodied worldview.*

From my linguistic studies background,[1] Wa Thiong'o's ideas reconnected me with "the Sapir-Whorf hypothesis." Which is: *a worldview colonizes every language.* Wa Thiong'o himself is indebted to linguists Edmund Sapir and Benjamin Whorf. I met Sapir and Whorf, through their writings, in graduate school.

---

[1] My doctoral dissertation at Northwestern University was on metaphor theory (1986).

Samuel Gyasi Obeng[2] links Whorfian linguistics to Wa Thiong'o's African appeal. Obeng writes: "According to Whorf, the structure of human language influences the manner in which human beings understand reality and behave with respect to it."[3] By "understand," the Whorffian hypothesis means "experiences."

Obeng cites Abiola Irele's argument in favor of returning to African languages. Irele, who teaches at Harvard[4], writes:

> "For even if it is true that all languages are systems whose reference to reality is arbitrary, there is a naturalization of particular languages to specific environments which plays an important role in the process by which they not only come to signify but *to achieve a correspondence with* the total configuration of the perceived and experienced reality within the environment."[5]

In a lecture at the University of Dar es Salaam, Wa Thiong'o stated his belief that "African leaders and scholars have become captives of their foreign languages, and so maintain colonial ideals to the detriment of fellow citizens."[6]

The African continent, says Thiong'o, continues to suffer from "language slavery." His proposal for escaping linguistic captivity is that "our local universities should translate the knowledge from foreign languages to local dialects for the benefits of all communities."[7]

---

[2] Professor of African Studies and Linguistics, University of Indiana.

[3] Samuel Gyasi Obeng, *Political Independence with Linguistic Servitude: The Politics About Languages in the Developing World* (London: Nova Science, 2002), pp. 98-99.

[4] Irele did his PhD at the University of Paris, and is an Associate of the Hutchins Center for African and African American Research, Harvard University, and Provost of the College of Humanities and Professor of French at Kwara State University.

[5] In Obeng, p. 99. Emphasis mine.

[6] "Foreign Tongues: Today's Slave Drivers," 11/23/13.

[7] Ib.

How deep, how radical (Latin *radix*; "root"), does this go? Wa Thiong'o "warned Africans against wasting their time and skills trying to change their accents to English; instead, they should spend their time and skills to protect African resources and language."[8]

The import of the Sapir-Whorf hypothesis is this: the language we use, not simply discrete words, but deep semantic and syntactic structures, becomes a framework that allows and disallows what we experience.

This has happened to the American Church. *The secular language of Westernization has colonized us.* This is not all good, since a colonizing language shapes what is and is not experienced. The result is that the typical Westernized Christian has been disenchanted and desacralized, to their ignorance.

For the presence-driven church to emerge from the ashes of secularization, we must be decolonized. A change in our church language can free us from the American Jesus, and from the consumer, theatric Church.[9]

In this chapter I am arguing for the following:

1) Language shapes reality.
2) The language we use delimits what we experience.
3) The Western Church has been colonized by the languages of entertainment, programs, "happiness," and quantitative-numerical ideas of "success"; thus,
4) A presence-driven church decolonizes the prevailing culture; which leads to
5) Increased experiential knowledge of the presence of God.

---

[8] Ib.

[9] See Stephen Prothero, *American Jesus: How the Son of God Became a National Icon* (New York: Farrar, Straus, and Giroux, 2003).

LANGUAGE SHAPES REALITY

The words we use are important. They frame the way we view reality. This affects how, and what, we experience. Words manifest a worldview; i.e., worldviews have their own language.

Strings of words, shaped into sentences and paragraphs, culminate in narratives that make a difference in our experience. Thus, a presence-driven church will take every word captive. Consider, for example, the word "success."

One indicator of world-conformation, hence infiltration and colonization, is the Church's quantification of Christianity. "Numbers" have become the measure of "success." This is not only about the heretical "prosperity gospel." Os Guinness writes:

> "America as the lead society in the modern world is awash with numbers and metrics, and with statistics, opinion polls, surveys, targets, pie charts, scorecards, big data, game theory and measurable outcomes—all at the expense of the true, the good, the beautiful, the faithful and the significant—and at the expense of God too. Numbers and the mania for metrics are therefore a critical element of secularization."[10]

In the Consumer Church, matters of the heart have been displaced by the number of hearts. Concerns of the soul have lost out to size of the building. The big questions now are "How many?" and "How much?" (The Church as a metaphysical Fitbit.) Guinness writes:

> "Nineteenth-century thinkers foresaw the rising domination of numbers, quantity and majority opinion, and warned against it. They regarded it as the overspill

---

[10] Os Guinness, *Renaissance: The Power of the Gospel However Dark the Times* (Downers Grove: InterVarsity, 2014), pp. 39-40.

of the age of democratic majorities and the triumph of technocratic rationalism, through which everything would be reduced to numbers, and big numbers would be valued most of all. The pressure would therefore be toward a false notion of explanation through numbers, a dangerous authority for numbers at the expense of the true and the good, and in the end toward a disastrous strengthening of the Leviathan of the state (for what else is "big" enough and "wise" enough to coordinate and manage everyone and everything but the government?)."[11]

Number-crunching is not irrelevant to the Church. But in the kingdom of God, numbers are not number 1.

"Success," American style, is usually thought of in quantitative, measurable terms. But the presence of God cannot be quantified and measured. Numbers do not say it all, or even much at all. Recall what happens in John 6:66, after Jesus shares a hard thing with his disciples. We read,

From this time many of his disciples turned back and no longer followed him.

That was a tough one. The formative church was shrinking in numbers! Jesus even challenges Peter, asking if he is going to leave as well. It's hard to think of many people leaving as "success." Yet, from a kingdom viewpoint, Jesus' mission was not compromised.[12]

I have chosen to substitute "obedience" for "success," since the latter is so freighted with Western consumerism. If "success" is used at all, it is redefined in terms of connectedness and obedience, not in numbers, size, and finances. Success, in the presence-driven church, cannot be quantified. Therefore, the vocabulary of the presence-driven church must differ from the program-driven church and the entertainment church.

---

[11] Ib., p. 40.

[12] I have a friend who had two thousand people leave his church (out of five thousand) after he preached a series of sermons on Jesus' words "My kingdom is not of this world."

Jesus is looking for "followers," not "attenders," and not even numerical "members." I have abandoned words like "attender," and "member." I replace these with "follower." Are my people following Jesus? Are they obedient? Are they connected to Jesus, like a branch connects to a vine? If so, that is a good sign.

In ideological warfare, it is not uncommon to remove certain words, and replace them with different words. There is a battle going on today in America over words and their meanings, such as "marriage." Words and sentences and paragraphs are mightier than guns and bombs in effecting culture change.

In George Orwell's *1984*, the main character, a man named Winston, has the responsibility of rewriting, or removing, history. In the process, Winston takes words, sentences, paragraphs, even narratives, and throws them into a "memory hole." Then, an alternative language is developed, called "newspeak." The result is that people slowly come to see and experience reality through the linguistic framework of newspeak. Underlying this is the belief that the language we speak shapes the reality we experience.

I have shared with colleagues that I have mostly abandoned the word "evangelical." Theologian Donald Dayton has done the same. Dayton writes:

> "I try to avoid the use of the word "evangelical" as much as possible. It is, in the words of British analytic philosophy, an "essentially contested concept" in which the basic meaning of the word is so in dispute that it is impossible to use it with precision or without participating in an ideological warfare that empowers one group over another."[13]

Dayton argues for a moratorium on the word "evangelical," because it has so many misleading connotations. These connotations function metaphorically, creating a framework through which people view the followers of Jesus.

---

[13] Quoted in Gary Black, *The Theology of Dallas Willard: Discovering Proto-Evangelical Faith* (Eugene, Oregon: Pickwick, 2013), p. 3.

In a similar way, I opt for a moratorium on the word "Christian." I use "Jesus-follower" instead. This is because, in my culture, "Christian" has many misleading and negative associations, and one of them is not "follower of Jesus as Lord."[14]

When the presence-driven church removes the word "success" from its vocabulary, there will come the slow death of the quantitative measurement tools of the Church Growth Movement. The Church Growth Movement arose in the late twentieth century. Gary Black describes it this way.

> "To track the quality of church membership, [Donald] McGavran suggested modern quantitative accounting methods to evaluate and measure specific determiners of church "success." Therefore, the CGM methodology gradually emphasized the accumulation, public reporting, and management of key metrics and measurements of congregational accomplishment."[15]

The Church Growth Movement focused on numbers – of new converts, of membership growth, of church service attendance, and of financial giving. Black writes that "Seeker Sensitive" or "Seeker Driven" churches are the logical and historical culmination of the Church Growth Movement. "If "crowds, cash, and converts" are growing, then successful contextualization of the gospel into the culture is believed to have occurred."[16]

The Seeker Church eventually morphed into the Entertainment Church, for that is its logical outcome. The Entertainment Church applies "the latest, modern consumer marketing techniques and technologies essential for displaying cultural acumen, creating an entertaining atmosphere, and maintaining brand loyalty in a competitive religious marketplace. The

---

[14] I am a Christian, and am thankful for it. But because the word is used in ways that have nothing to do with Christ in me, I'm using "Jesus-follower" instead. This is sad. What once was our word has been stolen by secular culture, redefined, and inserted back into culture.

[15] Black, p. 34.

[16] Ib., p. 35.

technology and marketing efforts focus directly on the Sunday morning "worship service.""[17]

Seeker-driven worship, at its quantitative worst, becomes the creation of a performance event, a spectacle, meant to entertain, for the sake of being successful. When a pastor succumbs to this, perhaps out of desperation for attendees, they commit what Eugene Peterson calls "vocational idolatry."[18]

Presence-driven churches are different than this. Numbers are not completely irrelevant. If you are a pastor of one hundred Jesus-followers, and this Sunday not one of them is in the house, God is trying to tell you something. But biblically, "presence" massively overwhelms "numbers." Keeping this clear heals the incessant guilt, shame, and pressure that accompany leaders in consumer-driven churches.

What if your church had but two, maybe three, followers of Jesus? The Consumer Church would consider that a massive disaster, because no one is buying your product. Jesus, however, does not view things that way. He says,

For where two or three gather in my name, there am I with them.[19]

Really? In the presence-driven church, better are three gathered in his name, than a thousand gathered elsewhere.

THE PRESENCE-DRIVEN PASTOR SPEAKS A DIFFERENT LANGUAGE

Mother Teresa once said, "I'm not called to be successful; I'm called to be faithful."[20]

---

[17] Ib.

[18] Eugene Peterson, *Under the Unpredictable Plant: An Exploration in Vocational Holiness* (Grand Rapids: Eerdmans, 1994), p. 4.

[19] Matthew 18:20.

[20] In Henri Nouwen, *Spiritual Formation: Following the Movements of the Spirit* (New York: HarperOne, 2015), p. 29.

As I hear her words, I resonate with them. Echoes of truth bounce off the chamber walls of my heart. I am freed from the vocational idolatry of the market-driven church, with its accompanying guilt and shame. Her words issue an invitation to view reality through a different lens, one that I find more biblical.

The words a pastor speaks to their people shape their hearts, and thus, their experience. Presence-driven words open doors to new ways of knowing God. This happens when "successful" is tossed down the memory hole, and the new way of speaking is "faithfulness."[21]

When a way of speaking changes, culture changes.[22] A church's culture will change from program-driven to presence-driven, as presence-driven leaders:

1) Live the Christ-abiding life themselves.
2) Lead their people into God's empowering presence.
3) Nurture and champion God-produced fruit-bearing.

As this happens, over time, the "language-game" of the church will change. When the language has changed, so does the experience.[23]

In my church, the following language shifts are taking place.

"Disciple" replaces "decider."

---

[21] In this case the new way of speaking is actually the old way. This is the resurrection of "faithfulness" from the dead.

[22] Consider, for example, the battle over defining "marriage."

[23] Something like this is happening when, in Mark 6, Jesus cannot perform many miracles in his home town. The people are using words like, "Isn't this the carpenter? Isn't this Mary's son and the brother of James, Joseph, Judas and Simon? Aren't his sisters here with us?" And they took offense at him." Here Jesus is reduced to a "carpenter." Later, some call Jesus "the Son of God." When the latter happens, one's experience of Jesus changes. Instead of seeing Jesus through the reductive lens of "carpenter," one now has a magnified vision of Jesus via "Son of God."

"Influence" replaces "numbers." The question is no longer, "How big is our church?" Instead, we ask, "What is our influence?" Biblically, influence is not in proportion to size.

"Abiding" replaces "striving." Abiding-language releases people from the guilt and pride associated with trying harder.

I use "doing" (deeds), but only after "abiding." This is the famous distinction between being and doing. In terms of ontological order, abiding precedes doing.

"Instruments of righteousness" replaces "tools for ministry." Here is the idea that God is forming us, like clay of a potter's wheel, into vessels that can contain his presence.

"Discernment" replaces "decision-making." This powerfully changes the religious atmosphere in a church. A paradigm shift takes place, in the sense that the most elementary thing we can do as Jesus' followers is listen for his voice, and follow.

"Voting" is thrown down the memory hole. "Discerning" is what matters. Because many vote, but few discern. This is not good for a church.

This eliminates the idea of "brainstorming." Instead of storming the gates of hell with our brains, we dwell in God's presence to discern our Shepherd's guiding voice. We assume God knows what he is doing. God has already decided. Our part is to discern what God has decided, rather than to decide for ourselves and assume this is what God desires.

I use "relationship," rather than "rules of order." This opens hearts up to the Hebraic idea that God loves us and is with us, even if only two or three are gathered. British parliamentary procedure is laid down, for the greatness of the Holy Spirit guiding our meetings. The Holy Spirit's name is not "Robert."[24]

---

[24] As in "Robert's Rules of Order."

"Follower" replaces "attendee." A presence-driven pastor views people by how their heart is formed, not in terms of their function. Formation prevails over function.

In our presence-driven church I constantly speak words like:

- Abiding
- Presence
- Listening
- Hearing
- Following
- Obedience
- Leading by being led
- Discerning
- Together
- Testifying
- Experiencing
- Formation
- Transformation
- Jesus-follower
- Worshiper
- Spirit-empowered
- Praying

These, and others, form a core vocabulary which shapes expectations. As Ruth Haley Barton writes:

> "Transforming community begins to emerge as we establish shared understanding about what spiritual transformation is, develop shared language for talking about and encouraging one another in the process, and embrace a shared commitment to arranging our lives for spiritual transformation."[25]

---

[25] Ruth Haley Barton, *Life Together in Christ: Experiencing Transformation in Community*, (Downers Grove: InterVarsity, 2014), Kindle Locations 133-134.

A shared language includes shared questions. The questions we ask shape the expectations we have. In the presence-driven church, we ask questions like this:

> What is God doing in your life?
> What is God saying to us, as a community?
> What does God want us to do?

This is not a theory, minus application. As a pastor, I *vocalize these sentences.* At times, on a Sunday morning, I ask our people, "What has God been doing in your life this past week?" The assumption is that God *has* been doing something. This opens the windows of the soul to the fresh air of faith. Things shift, spiritually, when people share testimonies of what God has been doing. Our people are encouraged; courage and hope displace fear and futility.

Not all churches ask these questions. In one of my seminary classes, a pastor raised his hand and confessed, with animation, "I attend a lot of meetings with many pastors. The question we ask is not, 'What does *God* think?' but, 'What do *you* think?'" This simple distinction seemed revolutionary for this pastor.

God-discourse is incendiary. Make these your core questions, and your ministry will change. Your people will begin to think in terms of them.[26]

The great Austrian philosopher Ludwig Wittgenstein once said, "The limits of my language mean the limits of my world." If Wittgenstein was right, then language is not so much a tool for recording and communicating information, but is the framework of all knowledge and experience.

When the Church gets colonized by a foreign worldview, presence-driven language and experience go down the memory-hole. A great forgetting takes

---

[26] In addition, authentic theologizing happens at this point. The question "What does God think?" raises core issues such as the nature of God, does God speak to us today, how can we hear the voice of God, and so on.

place. Psalm 44:20 reads: "If we had forgotten the name of our God, or spread out our hands to a foreign god, would not God have discovered it, since he knows the secrets of the heart?"

John Walton comments on this Orwellian possibility:

> "A deity's name, like Yahweh, is often associated with that god's power and essential being (Ex 3: 13– 14; Isa 9: 6). In Jeremiah 23:27, the false prophets plan to remove God's name from the people's memory so they will be enticed to follow Baal."[27]

In the presence-driven church a new language game is being played. People are enticed to follow God. They testify to tasting, and seeing, that the Lord is good. That which was desacralized emerges as sacred. The disenchanted becomes enchanted. Presence-driven churches have been decolonized from secular discourse. They speak a language that awakens experiential realities of the kingdom of God.

SUMMING UP – LEADERSHIP POINTS

Pastors and leaders – begin intentionally using presence-driven words and sentences. Systematically eliminate consumer and entertainment language.

In your leadership meetings, ask presence-driven questions.

Along the way, note how the new language is taking root, and how the old language is being uprooted. Pay attention to how this affects your people's expectations and testimonies.[28]

Expect that the decolonization/recolonization process will be a slow-cooker. Resist getting in the microwave. Instead, just simmer.

---

[27] NIV, Cultural Backgrounds Study Bible, Hardcover, Red Letter Edition: Bringing to Life the Ancient World of Scripture, (Grand Rapids: Zondervan, 2016), Kindle Locations 123378-123381).
[28] I see this happening in my church family.

8

LEADING THE PRESENCE-DRIVEN CHURCH

It is a hot, early fall Friday in Southeast Michigan. This morning I met with some of our leaders in my unofficial office at Panera Bread. We have begun the discerning process in preparation for our 2018 budget. The basic question is, "How does God want us to steward the resources he has placed in our care?" God is leading us to change some things, taking us in new directions.

I felt God give me some direction on the budget. I shared this with the others, presenting it as a proposal, so they could enter the discerning process with me. This is not a token offer granted to flatter, but how we do church.

Presence-driven leadership is not "top-down." It involves others. At Redeemer, we are not wedded to what the pastor wants, or how we have always done things. What happened to me six months ago illustrates this.

On Saturday morning, March 18, 2017, I woke early to travel from Monroe to downtown Detroit. I was speaking at a pastor's breakfast. My topic was, unsurprisingly, "Leading the Presence-Driven Church."

Sixty pastors were there. As I was speaking, I had a strong sense of God's presence. An anointing, upon the words I was saying. I saw it on the faces of the pastors. I sensed it as I prayed for them. Their response afterwards confirmed to me that God was meeting with us. God was taking ordinary, familiar words, and making them more than human words.

When the event was over, I felt filled, empowered, by God's Spirit. As I drove out of the parking lot God spoke to me.[1] I pulled over to the side and wrote these words: "John, do you realize what I have given you?" Probably not, since you asked.

I carried that little 3X5 card with me all day, and the next day, and for weeks afterwards. It was in my mind as I prepared to preach on Sunday. The text was 1 Peter 2:24.

> *"He himself bore our sins" in his body on the cross, so that we might die to*
> *sins and live for righteousness; "by his wounds you have been healed."*

We always take time to pray for the sick. On that day, God told me to call Sherry forward and pray for her. That was the day she was healed.

John, do you realize what God has given you? I could not get this out of my head! All that day, through the night, and when I awoke on Monday, I heard God asking this question. I heard it as I began preparing for the following Sunday's sermon on 1 Peter chapter 3.

1 Peter 3 is beautiful, on the husband-wife relationship. I love talking about marriages. But on that Monday, I could not get past three things: the question God asked me, the words "by his wounds we are healed," and Sherry's healing. Then, I knew. I discerned. God was telling me we were to camp around 1 Peter 2:24. For how long? As of today it's been six months, and God has not told us to move in a different direction.

On Sunday morning, March 26, I shared this with our church. I told how I felt God was speaking to me, and how I believed he was saying we are to stay with this one verse until he releases us. I wish you could have been with us that day! This is all my brothers and sisters want from me; viz., a

---

[1] Does God speak to us? See Dallas Willard, *Hearing God*, and my book *Praying*.

pastor who hears from God, and is willing to move with the Holy Spirit. The corporate discernment was confirming and empowering.

This exemplifies leadership in the presence-driven church. It's this:

1. Abide in Christ
2. Saturate in the Scriptures
3. Listen (Discern God's voice)
4. Obey

A.S.L.O.

It's not a real acronym, I know. At one of my conferences a pastor said it means, "Go as low as you can!" I like that.

In this chapter I present three things a presence-driven leader does. They are:

Presence-Driven Leaders Practice A.S.L.O.
Presence-Driven Leaders Teach A.S.L.O. to their people.
Presence-Driven Leaders Steward and Champion Transcendence.

I am sometimes asked, after doing these three things, what is the next step? My answer is: *there is no next step.* These are not "steps." They are more like a system. Cartoonist Scott Adams defined a system as "something you do on a regular basis that increases your odds of happiness in the long run."[2] Do these things, and you and your people will be blessed.

They run together, informing each other. They describe ongoing conditions of relationship. No one can predict what is coming down the road as these moments are lived, except that it will be good, and God will be magnified.

---

[2] Quoted in Adam Alter, *Irresistible: The Rise of Addictive Technology and the Business of Keeping Us Hooked*, (New York: Penguin, 2017) p. 117.

PRESENCE-DRIVEN PASTORS PRACTICE A.S.L.O.

The primary thing a presence-driven pastor does is dwell in God's presence. They resolutely abide in Christ. Then, they are led, by the Spirit. Presence-driven leaders lead by being led.[3]

"Dwelling in God's presence" is how the Old Testament expresses it. "Abiding in Christ" is the New Testament upgrade. In the Old Testament, we have "the presence of God," especially manifested in the tabernacle in the wilderness, and the Temple in Jerusalem. In the New Testament, we have "abiding in Christ," as given by Jesus, and our "in Christ" status in Paul's letters. In the New Testament, the presence motif gets more intimate, more intense. We become living temples, where God makes his home.

Before going to the cross, Jesus told his disciples about the coming upgrade. They are now to live connected to him, as their first act of being.

We hear Jesus' final leaderships instructions in John chapters 14-17. It is Easter week as he addresses his followers. The disciples are troubled. What, they wonder, will they do once their Master is gone? How is Jesus able to do the things he did? Jesus' response was crucial, and counterintuitive.

It was *crucial*, in that Jesus set before the disciples, and anyone who would follow him, the pattern of leadership foundational for the church. If the disciples don't do what Jesus says, they will fall away.[4] *Presence-driven leadership rises and falls on connectedness to Christ.*

It was *counterintuitive*. Jesus' leadership counsel goes against any leadership strategy the disciples ever heard. I doubt anyone could have anticipated what Jesus was about to say.

---

[3] See Henri Nouwen, *In the Name of Jesus: Reflections on Christian Leadership* (New York: Crossroad, 1989).
[4] John 16:1

It is instructive to note what he did not say. Regarding the origin of his supernatural activity, Jesus did not counsel us to form committees and figure things out on our own. Nor did he say, "I did such great things because I worked really hard." Instead, Jesus put forth something that sounds mystical, and impractical. "I did what I did, because I am in the Father, and the Father is in me."

Say what?! Jesus' authoritative words, healings, deliverances, and dead raisings, were possible because he indwelt the Trinitarian personhood of God.[5] Here Jesus gets ontological. He's going deeper than any fisherman ever lowered his nets.

That may have been fine for Jesus, but what about us? The answer he gives his disciples must have stunned them. They, he reveals, are invited to share in God's Trinitarian being, with all its resources.[6]

Like a connected branch shares the nutrients of the vine, a disciple connected to Jesus shares in the life-giving flow of peace and joy that transcends this world's happiness. Experientially, the peace and joy that has existed everlastingly between Father, Son, and Spirit, can be ours.

Within the vast spaces of this super-reality, real church happens. A presence-driven pastor relocates here. Here is where presence-driven leadership begins, and remains. How do you lead a presence-driven church? *Do this: stay connected.*

The promise is, as we abide in Christ, we will do the things Jesus did, and even greater things. I have heard sermons on the promised "greater things." While that excites me, I confess to simply desiring the things Jesus did; viz., heal the sick, raise the dead, deliver the oppressed, and speak words of authority that bring people into God's kingdom.

---

[5] See Stephen Seamands, *Ministry In the Image of God: The Trinitarian Shape of Christian Service* (Downers Grove: Intervarsity, 2006).

[6] See John Ortberg, "Experiential Knowledge of the Trinity." In Dallas Willard, *Living in Christ's Presence: Final Words on Heaven and the Kingdom of God.*

This is the key to the Presence-Driven Church. Jesus said:

> *Remain in me, as I also remain in you. No branch can bear fruit by itself; it must remain in the vine. Neither can you bear fruit unless you remain in me.*

> *"I am the vine; you are the branches. If you remain in me and I in you, you will bear much fruit; apart from me you can do nothing.*[7]

This is the New Testament upgrade to the presence motif. It is the new reality of full intimacy with God.[8] How close can we get? John Jefferson Davis writes:

> "The believer is really, truly, factually, ontologically united in communion with all three persons of the triune God, Father, Son and Holy Spirit. This truth of the believer's new state of being precedes and is the proper foundation of any particular act of worship."[9]

As followers of Jesus, we have a new ontological status. The nature of our identity, our being, has changed. The core concept the apostle Paul is trying to get the early church to realize and understand is this: now, they are "in Christ." Christ, the hope of glory, resides in them. This is central to how we are to understand ourselves, and why Paul uses the "in Christ" metaphor, and variations of it (e.g., "through Christ," "with Christ"), 216 times.[10]

Davis describes the intimate connection.

---

[7] John 15:4-5

[8] By "full intimacy" I do not mean metaphysical union, as Meister Eckhart seems at times to approach.

[9] Davis, *Worship and the Reality of God: An Evangelical Theology of Real Presence*, Kindle Locations 745-746.

[10] See Constantine Campbell, *Paul and Union with Christ*, (Grand Rapids: Zondervan, 2012). Campbell examines every occurrence of the phrases 'in Christ', 'with Christ', 'through Christ', 'into Christ,' and other related expressions, exegeting each passage in context and taking into account the unique lexical contribution of each Greek preposition.

"As Herman Ridderbos has astutely noted, the mystical union, being "in Christ," is not just an occasional reality in certain sublime spiritual moments; rather it is, in Pauline and New Testament teaching, "an abiding reality determinative for the whole of the Christian life.... we have to do here with the church's 'objective' state of salvation." We are as really connected to Christ and to other believers by the bond of the Holy Spirit as teenagers, texting one another other on their cell phones, are connected to one another by the invisible signals broadcast from the nearest cell tower."[11]

Constantine Cambell says the Pauline "metatheme of *union, participation, identification, incorporation is. . . the essential ingredient that binds all other [Pauline] elements together.*"[12]

The presence-driven pastor, as their first order of life and leadership, abides in Christ. They live in constant connectedness. This includes saturation in The Narrative.[13] They listen for the guiding voice of God. They obey.

Presence-driven pastors do this well. Without this, they are irrelevant and inauthentic. Disconnected branches produce nothing for Christ. They have fallen away from God's presence.

The pastor-as-connected-branch lives up close and personal with the trunk of the tree. Fruit-bearing nutrients ooze into them. The properties of the tree just are the properties of the branch. In the same way, properties of God are shared with the connected human heart, which then "bears fruit." These

---

[11] Ib., Kindle Locations 748-751

[12] Campbell, *op. cit.*, p. 9.

[13] By "The Narrative" I mean the Christian scriptures. See N.T. Wright's *Scripture and the Authority of God*, on Scripture as a Narrative in five acts.

include the God-properties of love, peace, patience, kindness, gentleness, and self-control.[14]

The final piece of A.S.L.O. is obedience. We lead, by being led. We are led, as we abide in God's presence. We discern what God calls us to do, and then we follow.

This is the job description for presence-driven pastors and leaders. This is so radical, so revolutionary, so pregnant with possibilities, that leadership shares it with their people. This is the second ongoing condition of presence-driven leadership.

THE PRESENCE-DRIVEN PASTOR TEACHES A.S.L.O. TO THEIR PEOPLE

Linda and I sat in the restaurant booth across from the young couple that was checking out our church. They left their consumer-driven church in the Detroit area. After years serving there, they had burned out. When we met, the fire inside them was reduced to an ember.

The husband seemed tense as he asked me, "If we come to your church, what are you going to expect us to do?"

I responded, "Nothing."

Nothing?

"Correct. We will, however, teach you to abide in Christ, and to discern the voice of God. God will then show you what you are to do, and when you are to do it."

---

[14] The biblical "fruit of the Spirit" in Galatians 5:22-23 are the properties of God, born in us. God does not share all his properties with us, such as his omniscience and omnipotence. But it is arguable that God shares his omnibenevolence with us. On this see Wayne Grudem's distinction between "communicable" and "incommunicable" attributes of God, in his *Systematic Theology*.

After all their years in a church, they had never heard of such a thing. I have had this response from several seminary students and pastors over the years.

The presence-driven pastor teaches their people how to abide in Christ. They bring them into the perichoretic Trinitarian being of God. They know, from experience and The Text, that the number one thing Jesus-followers and communities need is God, as an experiential reality. Out of their own intimate, relational familiarity with God and God's Spirit, presence-driven pastors introduce their people to the presence of God, and the abiding life in Christ.

In Ephesians 4:11 the Greek word for "pastor" is *poimenos*. Literally translated, it means "shepherd." Pastors shepherd their people into the green pastures and still waters of God's lavish, boundless presence. Their people are taught to be "branches," connected to Jesus, the True Vine. As this happens, much "fruit" comes forth.

A pastor cultivates this in their people by introducing them to The Connected Life. This includes teaching how to hear the voice of God. I teach our people how to hear God's voice like this:

1. Abide in Christ.
2. Saturate in the Scriptures.
3. Hang around people who do 1 and 2.

Eugene Peterson describes his life as a shepherd of people this way.

> "God and passion. That is why I was a pastor, that is why I had come to this place: to live in the presence of God, to live with passion — and to gather others into the presence of God, introducing them into the possibilities of a passionate life."[15]

---

[15] Eugene Peterson, *Under the Unpredictable Plant: An Exploration in Vocational Holiness* (Grand Rapids: Eerdmans, 1992), p. 45.

In the spiritual classic *The Practice of the Presence of God*, Brother Lawrence writes, "If I were a preacher, I would preach nothing but practicing the presence of God." This is because everything is available in God's presence.

This is what Jesus taught his disciples. He didn't tell them to study hard (though we ought to study hard); he didn't tell them to work hard (even though we are to work hard at all he gives us to do); and he didn't tell them to be busy all the time. Jesus did tell his disciples to *rest in him*. Primordially.

Presence-driven pastors lead their people to rest in Christ. The presence-driven pastor abides in Christ, and shows, by example and teaching, how to enter into relationship with the Trinitarian God. The pastor and their people become an abiding church. This becomes their identity, out of which all else emerges. Presence-driven leaders champion this.

PRESENCE-DRIVEN PASTORS ARE STEWARDS AND CHAMPIONS OF TRANSCENDENCE

When Rylee graduated from Monroe High School she went to Ferris State University, a four hour drive from home.[16] Rylee was a follower of Jesus. But, like many incoming freshmen, she disconnected from her faith and fell into a party lifestyle.

I remember the Sunday morning Rylee came home, physically and spiritually. She was at a party on campus on a Saturday night. Things were happening to her, and she was making choices, that made her afraid. She was in trouble, and called her brother in Monroe. "Can you come get me and bring me home?!"

Rylee's brother left Monroe, arriving at Ferris State in the middle of the night. They packed all her stuff and came straight to our 10:30 worship event.

---

[16] "Rylee" is not her real name. I was in campus ministry at Michigan State University, and have seen this story happen countless times.

A few of us knew she was coming and were waiting to welcome her home. She came to me and said, with tears in her eyes, "I would like people to pray for me. May we do that?"

Our worship team was playing as Rylee and I walked to the front of the sanctuary. "Rylee is asking for prayer." Then she spoke through the tears, sharing her story. "She wants prayer this morning," I said. I felt led by the Spirit to invite women to come forward, surround her, and pray for her. Many came. I remember thinking, "This... is church!"

Then I felt God say to me, "Invite any girls who are struggling like Rylee to come forward and pray for them." A few girls came. Others surrounded them. The thought came, "You won't be preaching today."

God was orchestrating our gathering. It was powerful, beautiful, loving. It was the activated body of Christ, ministering as we have taught them to. It was more memorable than my preaching. Actually, it preached better than my preaching.

In this chapter I am arguing for presence-driven leadership as three ongoing, concurrent conditions. They could be stated this way.

> Presence-driven leaders tend the fire within (practice A.S.L.O.).
>
> Presence-driven leaders bring the fire to their people (teach A.S.L.O.).
>
> Presence-driven leaders tend the burning fire (discern, steward, champion, and facilitate what God is doing).

I was tending the fire when we prayed for Rylee and the other girls. God was moving. I drew attention to this by speaking to our people as the prayers were happening. "God," I said, "is doing a great thing in Rylee and in us this morning. We are going to let it happen. It's better than anything we could have anticipated." And my people, because they have been so trained, agreed.

The movement of God's Spirit is a felt, discernible thing. Leaders must nurture and cultivate God's presence, in their community. We must be very, very open to it. We must take care that we stay vertical.

John Calvin, who is often inaccurately portrayed as being spiritually cold and aloof, had as his emblem a flaming heart with an outstretched hand. On it was the motto, *Cor meum quasi immolatum tibi offero, Domine* - "I give my flaming heart to you, Lord, eagerly and honestly."

Calvin had these words carved over the pulpit in Geneva where he preached. Alvin Plantinga writes:

> Of the Holy Spirit, [Calvin] says that "persistently boiling away and burning up our vicious and inordinate desires, he enflames our hearts with the love of God and with zealous devotion." The *Institutes* are throughout aimed at the practice of the Christian life (which essentially involves the affections), not at theological theory; the latter enters only in the service of the former."[17]

Presence-driven leaders fan into flame the gift of God, which is the Holy Spirit manifested in power, love, and self-discipline.[18] Practically, I do this by...

> ... inviting people to share testimonies of what God is doing in their lives. I help people put their stories together, in five-minute packages. Some share how God has healed them. Others share how God has guided them, or provided for them. We do this on Sunday mornings. And, I send testimonies by email to our people.

---

[17] Alvin Plantinga, *Knowledge and Christian Belief*, p. 72. Plantinga is referring to Calvin's *Institutes of the Christian Religion*.
[18] 2 Timothy 1:6-7.

… regularly calling for one-sentence testimonies when we gather as a community on Sunday mornings. I'll say, e.g., "Please share, in one sentence, what you do to connect with Jesus during the week." Or, "Please share, in a sentence, something God has done for you this past week." Whenever I do this, many of our people share.

… laying hands on people and anointing them with oil. As Paul told Timothy in 2 Timothy 1:6, *I remind you to fan into flame the gift of God, which is in you through the laying on of my hands.* I'll call people forward who want this. I'll say, e.g., "I bless you with power, love, and self-discipline." Or, "I bless you with a fresh impartation of the power of the Holy Spirit."

… discerning what I see God doing during a Sunday morning gathering. This often happens as we are worshiping. I step forward and share this with the people. I might say, "I sense God's love and pleasure falling upon us." Or, "I see God giving new hope to some here who came worried about the future."

Presence-driven leaders sense and discern what God is doing among their people, and get behind it. They lift it up, and thank God for what he is doing, presently. In this they throw another log on the already consuming fire of God's presence.

I like how James MacDonald writes about this.

"Transcendence is the best single word I have found to describe the attributes of God that are found only in Him and what is missing too often from our churches. We are facilitators of transcendence. Our main job is to usher in the Almighty— God forgive us when we have settled for less. When transcendence is welcomed and unveiled, no one even notices the program, the preacher, or other people. Anything resembling performance seems out of place. Because all that is visible is eclipsed by what is not: God Himself moving through the church in power and meeting with His people in manifest ways."[19]

Presence-driven leaders notice and facilitate transcendence. They spiritually discern. They can do this because they live connected to God. They share their experiential knowledge with their people. They become scholars of God's presence. They recognize God when he is moving, and draw attention to it. They understand none of this can be predicted or programmed, and they explain this to their people. This is all about relationship, connection, being with God, and with people.

Presence-driven leaders shepherd God's people into God's presence. Beyond that, they don't know what to predict, except that it will be good, and fruitful.

SUMMING UP – LEADERSHIP POINTS

1. This book presents A.S.L.O. as the key to leadership in a presence-driven church. Agree or disagree? Discuss this with your leaders.
2. Leadership in the Presence-Driven Church looks like this:
   a. The pastor/leader practices, as a lifestyle, A.S.L.O.
   b. The pastor/leader teaches their people to do the same.
   c. The pastor/leader steward and facilitates transcendence. Using these three guidelines, evaluate yourself and encourage your leaders to do the same.
3. Pastors — focus on your connectedness to Jesus. Engage in the spiritual disciplines, as entrees into the presence of God. Make this central to your life and ministry.
4. Read, study, and apply the guidance in books like:
   a. *The Contemplative Pastor*, by Eugene Peterson

---

[19] James MacDonald, *Vertical Church: What Every Heart Longs For, What Every Church Can Be*, Kindle Locations 498-502.

b. *In the Name of Jesus*, by Henri Nouwen

c. *A Celebration of Discipline*, by Richard Foster

d. *Strengthening the Soul of Your Leadership*, by Ruth Haley Barton

e. *Praying*, by John Piippo

5. Keep a spiritual journal, as a record of the voice and activity of God in your life.

6. Teach your staff how to do this. At staff meetings, have people share from their journals, responding to the question, "How has God's presence been real for you since we last met?"

7. Allow for people to share testimonies when the church gathers. After a testimony, vocally highlight God's presence and what you see God doing.

9

GOD'S PRESENCE WILL WIN THE DAY

The first time I saw Kerry[1] he was walking past the coffee shop. I had not seen him in Monroe before. Kerry is tall, covered with tattoos, with hair going down to his waist. I was drawn to him. God was placing him on my heart.

Two weeks later I was driving south on Telegraph Road in a pouring rain. Telegraph is one of the Detroit area's busiest roads. Before I-75 was built, it was called "bloody Telegraph" because of the many accidents. Ahead of me on the right I saw Kerry, with his arm outstretched and his thumb in the air. He was hoping for a ride. No one was taking his offer.

God told me, "Pick him up."

I pulled into a parking lot and circled back to where Kerry was standing. I signaled for him to get in my car. He was drenched as he asked me, "Why'd you do that? Why'd you pick me up?"

"Because," I said, "God told me to."

"I don't believe in God."

"Well, I do. So, I picked you up."

---

[1] Not his real name.

Kerry was going to a friend's apartment, where he was staying. I eventually learned that Kerry was a musician, a singer, a front man for a thrash metal band that once played with the band Slayer. Kerry is a phenomenal vocalist with a four-octave range. And, as he told me, he struggles with alcohol.[2]

We arrived at the apartment, and I asked Kerry if I could pray for him. "I don't believe in prayer," he said. "Well, I do. So, I am going to pray for you."

As I prayed for Kerry, I felt God was showing me his heart, and that it was good. I said, "Kerry, God is showing me that you have a good heart." With those words Kerry began to cry, placed his head on my shoulder, and said, "I *do* have a good heart."

I gave Kerry my phone number. Two week later I saw him again, on Telegraph Road.

He was sitting on the curb on the northbound lane, with his head down. I pulled into a lot and walked over to him.

"Kerry, what's going on? How are you doing?"

"I'm thinking about walking into the traffic."

"Kerry, you can't do that! Come with me, please!"

As we were driving back to the apartment, I told him about God's love for him, and how God changed my life. God wanted to change Kerry, and give him a new life in the beautiful kingdom.

"Kerry," I said, "I would love to have you visit my church family."

"They wouldn't want me there."

"Yes, they would, Kerry. My church isn't like other places."

---

[2] I had problems with drugs and alcohol before I became a follower of Jesus.

As I dropped Kerry off that day, I was certain Kerry would never set foot in our church building. But I was wrong.

The next weekend came, and we were having a Sunday night worship evening. Our worship musicians come together, and we just spend time in God's presence, praising him. With no other agenda, except what the Spirit desires.

I was playing guitar on the worship team that evening. I'm an old rock guitarist who used to teach at Rick Nielsen's father's guitar studio in Rockford, Illinois.[3] I often play with my eyes closed. At one point I opened them, and saw Kerry, sitting in the last row of the sanctuary. My heart rate elevated, as did my spirit. He came! I was filled with hope, and joy, and some fear as I wondered what Kerry would think of my guitar playing. I was relieved when later Kerry told me, "John, you can thrash!"

I closed my eyes, now praying as I was playing. When I opened them again Kerry was no longer in the last row. He had come forward, and was sitting in the front row, his head down.

Kerry sat there for several minutes. Then, he got up and walked out of the sanctuary. I put my guitar down and followed him.

"Kerry, I'm so glad you came. What's going on?"

Kerry said, "Something is happening inside of me."

"What is it, Kerry? Is it good?"

"O yeah, it's good. I feel like I am being purged."

"That's God, Kerry. He is moving inside your heart!"

---

[3] Rick Nielsen eventually formed the band "Cheap Trick."

Kerry sometimes slept under the bridges in Monroe. That night we put him up in the Knight's Inn. When morning came I called to see how he was doing. He said, "John, come over. I have something to tell you."

I arrived at the Knight's Inn, went to Kerry's room, and he told me he slept that night, alcohol free, for the first time in a long time. He looked at me and said, "John, I had a dream last night. I dreamed you and I were under bridges rescuing people."

"Kerry," I responded, "God is revealing his plans and purposes to you! God is going to use you to rescue people in your death metal culture!"

"Yeah, God could never use you to rescue people like me."

With those words, I just smiled. And was filled with joy.

I love Kerry. Kerry loves me, and Linda, too. He lives thirty miles from us. We communicate through Facebook, sometimes by phone, and we've gone to Detroit to visit with him.

Kerry has told me that he loves Jesus. He got an online certificate to be a pastor. He does ministry in the death metal community. Like me, Kerry is a work in progress. Also like me, his life in Christ began with a powerful experience, and encounter, with the living God.

In this chapter I make the claim that, despite the entrenched consumerism and secularism in Western culture, churches that are presence-driven will flourish. I believe where the presence of God is experienced, God's kingdom will bloom.[4] People of all kinds and cultures, like Kerry, will be persuaded.

---

[4] My strategy is different than Rod Dreher's *The Benedict Option*. I agree with Dreher that the Church in America has lost the culture war. Dreher is looking for a new "Benedict." I am looking for new "Moseses" (see, e.g., Exodus 33:15; see N.T. Wright's core idea that, in Jesus, we are seeing a new Exodus). Dreher and I both agree that, for the Church to survive in Western culture, things must drastically change.

This is because nothing on earth, or off the earth, is like God's empowering presence. Money cannot buy it. You cannot program it. It is not for our entertainment. Nothing compares, nothing competes with, the felt reality of God with us.

A long time ago, in what seems like an eternity to me, Linda and I gathered with brothers and sisters who were born out of The Jesus Movement[5], and sang songs like "Pass It On." We worshiped to the idea that God's love is something to be experienced and, once you have experienced it, you want to pass it on to others.

Once you've experienced it. I believed it then, and I believe it now. The spark is God's presence. The fire is his emergent kingdom. Once again, for such a time as this, God's presence what is needed to win the day.

In almost every turn of the pages in the Bible I encounter God's presence. When I woke this morning, I went to my home office and opened to Psalms. I have been stuck on Psalm 88:12-14 for three days. Today I wrote these verses on a 3X5 card, placed it in my pocket, and kept it close to me.

> *The righteous will flourish like a palm tree,*
> *they will grow like a cedar of Lebanon;*
> *planted in the house of the LORD,*
> *they will flourish in the courts of our God.*
> *They will still bear fruit on old age. . .*

The logic of this promise is:

My church is planted in the house of the Lord.
We will flourish in the courts of our God.
We will bear fruit, even in old age.

---

[5] See Larry Eskridge, *God's Forever Family: The Jesus People Movement in America* (Cambridge: Oxford University Press, 2013).

I hear this promise echoing through the halls of Scripture. The fruit-bearing will come from the presence of Christ, in us. The fulfillment and meaning we experience will be a banquet table, overflowing onto a different presence, that of our enemies. God will affect them, because what they most need, whether acknowledged or not, is to be awakened to what Dallas Willard called the "most real thing in existence"; viz., the Trinitarian presence of God.[6]

The most real thing in existence has not gone away. On this truth, I anchor my claim that God's presence will win the day.

THE METAPHYSICAL IMPULSE IS NOT GOING AWAY

This fall I began my eighteenth year of teaching philosophy of religion at Monroe County Community College.[7] In the first class, I introduce students to the abstract, hyper-logical, Ontological Argument for God's Existence.[8] Most are shocked, intrigued, even delighted by the argument. It comes at you like a puzzle, which, once understood, elicits several "Ahas!"

My students are interested in the Ontological Argument. They want to talk about it. They want to disagree with it. They want to agree with it. To do either, they must first understand it. Atheists cannot believe the argument works. Theists believe they now have justification for their faith. Consistently, over the years, I have seen students willingly and actively engage with the possibility of God. It will happen with my new students this fall. Why? Answering this question will tell us much about the power of a presence-driven church.

---

[6] See Dallas Willard, *Living in Christ's Presence: Final Words on Heaven and the Kingdom of God*, Chapter 9, "Experiential Knowledge of the Trinity."

[7] In Monroe, Michigan.

[8] I teach Anselm's version. Sometimes I also teach the Modal Version of the Ontological Argument. It is more powerful than Anselm's because, for one reason, it avoids Kant's criticism that "exists" is not a predicate.

Students are energized by the God-talk in my philosophy of religion classes. This is because all of them, whether they realize it or not, are created in the image of God.[9] God is their heavenly Father, and they cannot escape him. They are children of God, owe their existence to God, are created to know and worship God, and are destined to find their meaning and purpose in intimacy with God.

This God desire has not gone away. It cannot go away, because we are made in God's image.[10] I see it in atheist Julian Barnes's opening words in his book *Nothing to Be Frightened Of*. He confesses, "I don't believe in God, but I miss him."[11]

I call this the *metaphysical impulse*. J. P. Moreland calls it *the recalcitrant imago dei*.[12] A "recalcitrant" fact is one that is stubborn, and will not go away, despite attempts to explain it away. Moreland writes:

> "The Bible teaches that human beings are made in the image of God. This implies that there are things about our make-up that are like God is. At the beginning of his *Institutes of the Christian Religion*, John Calvin observed: "No man can survey himself without forthwith turning his thoughts towards the God in whom he lives and moves; because it is perfectly obvious, that the endowments which we possess cannot possible be from ourselves..."[13]

---

[9] Not all students are captivated by the arguments for and against God. But most are. That is my consistent observation. My students are not graded on whether they believe in God or not, but on their understanding of the philosophical arguments. One cannot evaluate, for or against, until one understands. Understanding precedes evaluation. Many of my students have come to believe in God while in my classes.

[10] If it is true that all persons have been made in God's image, then, *ipso facto*, God-desire will not go away. Even if some atheists claim to have no God-desire.

[11] Julian Barnes, *Nothing to Be Frightened Of* (New York: Alfred Knopf, 2008), p. I.

[12] J. P. Moreland, *The Recalcitrant Imago Dei: Humans and the Failure of Naturalism* (London: SCM Press, 2009).

[13] Ib., p. 4

I see in my philosophy students a longing for God, a yearning for the transcendent. Theologian John Jefferson Davis sees the same yearning in video-gamers. He writes:

> "[The video game] World of Warcraft is an impressive contemporary example of a game as defined by [Johan] Huizinga: "a voluntary activity ... executed within certain fixed limits ... having its aim in itself... and *the consciousness that it is different from ordinary life.*"[14]

For some, games like World of Warcraft function as a substitute for religion. They partially satisfy the thirst engendered by the metaphysical impulse.

In ancient Israel, this deep yearning found relief in the Jerusalem temple. Psalm 84:4 says, "Blessed are those who dwell in your house; they are ever praising you." Commenting on this verse, John Walton writes:

> "Being constantly in deity's presence is considered a privilege to be longed for throughout the ancient Near East. The Babylonian king Neriglissar expresses to his god that he wants to be where his god is forever. Another text requests that the king might stand before the god forever in adoration. The Hymn to Marduk requests that the worshiper may stand before the deity forever in prayer, supplication and entreaty. In the third millennium BC, Sumerian worshipers tried to accomplish this objective by placing statuettes of themselves in the posture of prayer in the temple. In this way they would be continuously represented in the temple."[15]

---

[14] John Jefferson Davis, *Worship and the Reality of God: An Evangelical Theology of Real Presence*, Kindle Locations 1104-1105. Emphasis mine.
[15] John Walton and Craig Keener, *NIV, Cultural Backgrounds Study Bible*, Kindle Location 249745.

We see the ancient impulse in Psalm 63:1-5.

You, God, are my God,
earnestly I seek you;
I thirst for you,
my whole being longs for you,
in a dry and parched land
where there is no water.
² I have seen you in the sanctuary
and beheld your power and your glory.
³ Because your love is better than life,
my lips will glorify you.
⁴ I will praise you as long as I live,
and in your name I will lift up my hands.
⁵ I will be fully satisfied as with the richest of foods

Tom Schwanda says this psalm communicates "the intense longing and fulfilled delight of being in God's presence."[16]

The metaphysical impulse is expressed in C.S. Lewis's Argument from Desire for the Existence of God.[17] God, reasoned Lewis, is the best explanation of the human desire for the transcendent and the permanent. Joe Puckett explains:

> "Nearly nine out of every ten people living harbor some variety of religious belief. Though the beliefs themselves differ widely, a common thread is the conviction of some metaphysically and axiologically ultimate reality that infuses human existence with meaning and determines the nature and course of the human Good Life."[18]

---

[16] Tom Schwanda, *Journal of Spiritual Formation and Soul Care*, Spring 2014, Volume 7, No. I, p. 70.

[17] See Joe Puckett, *The Apologetics of Joy: A Case for the Existence of God from C.S. Lewis's Argument from Desire*, Eugene, Oregon: Wipf and Stock, 2012).

[18] Ib., Kindle Location 60.

There is a great longing in the human heart for something more. For something beyond us, that will complete us. We see this in the Psalms.

My soul yearns, even faints, for the courts of the Lord;
my heart and my flesh cry out for the living God.
Psalm 84:1

O God, you are my God, earnestly I seek you;
my soul thirsts for you, my body longs for you.
Psalm 63: 1

One thing have I desired of the Lord, that I will seek after;
that I . . . behold the beauty of the Lord.
Psalm 27: 4

As the deer pants for streams of water, so my soul pants for you, O God.
My soul thirsts for God, for the living God.
Ps. 42: 1-2

I open my mouth and pant, longing for your commands.
Ps. 119: 131

"Panting" for God is a manifestation of the deep, existential thirst for something, Someone, who will explain and fulfill us. In *The Weight of Glory* C.S. Lewis wrote:

"We do not want merely to see beauty, though, God knows, even that is bounty enough. We want something else which can hardly be put into words — to be united with the beauty we see, to pass into it, to receive it into ourselves, to bathe in it, to become part of it."[19]

---

[19] C.S. Lewis, *The Weight of Glory* (New York: HarperOne, 2001), p. 8.

Alvin Plantinga expands on this. He writes:

> "This love for God isn't like, say, an inclination to spend the afternoon organizing your stamp collection. It is longing, filled with desire and yearning; and it is physical as well as spiritual: "my body longs for you, my soul pants for you." Although *eros* is broader than sexual love, it is analogous to the latter. There is a powerful desire for *union* with God, the oneness Christ refers to in John 17."[20]

This powerful desire is *the recalcitrant metaphysical impulse*. It just won't go away.

How is it satisfied? Famously, Augustine wrote that the human heart will be restless until it finds its rest in God. *This is why only God's presence can win.* Presence-driven churches will provide the answer to the unspoken cries of humanity living in the waterless wasteland of horizontal, secular culture.

GOD'S PRESENCE WINS THE DAY

One of my favorite cartoonists is Gary Larson. I have many of his cartoon collection books. I wish he would come out of retirement and draw again!

One cartoon shows two panelists and a game host. They are playing "Jeopardy." One contestant is named Norman. The other is God, complete with long white hair and beard, rays of bright glory streaming from his essence. The caption reads:

> "Yes! That's right! The answer is 'Wisconsin'! Another 50 points for God, and, uh-oh..., looks like Norman, our current champion, hasn't even scored yet."

Norman had no chance against God. Neither does secularism and consumerism. Nothing this world serves up can compare, or compete with, God.

[20] Alvin Plantinga, *Knowledge and Christian Belief*, p. 75.

In the end, God wins. This present age will be consumed in the fiery, apocalyptic love of God. Then begins the age to come, which is God's kingdom, fully instantiated, present, and accounted for.

When we pray for God to let his kingdom come, on earth, as it is in heaven, God brings his winning essence into this fallen world. Presently, in this present darkness, where God's presence is, he overcomes.

When God's kingdom comes, things are on earth as they are in heaven. Wherever God's presence is, he reigns. The light of God overrules and overwhelms darkness. Always. It transforms have-nots into haves, nones into somes, nobodies into somebodies, and skeptics into believers. I know, because that was me.

God's presence is what wins the day. Not talk, but power. At a conference years ago, Dallas Willard placed a sign on the wall that said, "The [human] will is transformed by experience, not information."[21] When Jesus walks into the room, everything changes. He comes with more than a lecture to establish his kingdom. His presence is transforming.

This past Sunday, I took my rotation teaching our third through fifth graders. When class was over, I walked the hallway from our children's wing to our sanctuary. When I stepped into the sanctuary, I saw people at the altar. Many were praying for them. I looked, and saw old and young, who were still there. It felt electric. God was present and winning, in us!

A teen-aged girl was crying, held by the aunt who brought her that morning. I went to her and asked, "Is God doing a good thing in you?" She nodded her head, and said, "Yes." I asked if I could pray for her. Yes, she said, through tears of transformation. As I prayed, God was giving me words to confirm and address her condition.[22]

---

[21] Dallas Willard, *Living in Christ's Presence: Final Words on Heaven and the Kingdom of God*, p. 56.
[22] I Corinthians 12:8, "To one there is given through the Spirit a message of wisdom, to another a message of knowledge by means of the same Spirit..."

A young woman was walking back from the altar, assisted by her cane. A broad smile spread from cheek to cheek. She sat in her chair, and just hung around, taking it all in. She texted me today, saying, "I cannot wait for next Sunday!"

I asked a young man who was visiting, "How was this morning for you?" "Like drinking," he replied, "from a firehose."

An older woman, one of our long-time members, wrote these words on a Facebook post today: "God's blessing and anointing is on Redeemer!"

When love and power come down from heaven, people stay. A.W. Tozer said, "It is not mere words that nourish the soul, but God himself, and unless and until the hearers find God in personal experience, they are not better for having heard the truth."[23] Last Sunday at Redeemer, many were better for having been met by God.

Think of it like this. If God showed up in your church, if "surely the Lord is in our place,"[24] and your people knew it, would not this singular fact interest seekers, skeptics, agnostics, and "nones"? I see this happening, again and again.

My thesis is that all our business, marketing, and entertainment strategies unravel before the presence of God. This is Church as a movement, not an institution, inhabited and led by God.

Without God, we lose. A consumer-driven focus is not working, and only adds to our longing.[25] Only God's presence can win the day. And, ultimately, it will.

---

[23] A. W. Tozer, *The Pursuit of God*, Kindle Location 53.

[24] Genesis 28:16, "When Jacob awoke from his sleep, he thought, "Surely the Lord is in this place, and I was not aware of it."

[25] See Rod Dreher, "Trump Can't Save American Christianity." *The New York Times*, August 2, 2017. See also Italian atheist philosopher Marcello Pera, in *Why We Should Call Ourselves Christians: The Religious Roots of Free Societies* (New York: Encounter, 2008). Pera argues that Europe will only be saved from its cultural demise if it returns to Christianity.

Presence-driven churches understand the word "in."[26] *In* God. *In* Christ. This is my weary soul's resting place, my hungry soul's banquet, my thirsty spirit's living water. The presence-driven church addresses the deepest waters of the human heart. Greg Boyd writes:

> "Our deepest hunger is only satisfied when we're rightly related to God. Only our Creator can give us the fullness of Life we crave. Why did God create us with this hunger? Because he wants to share himself with us. He wants us to participate in his divine nature (1 Peter 1:4). As Father, Son, and Holy Spirit, he longs for us to join in his eternal dance of perfect, ecstatic love... The Trinity is our home, and we are never fully satisfied or at peace until we rest in him."[27]

What happened in the spring of 1970 still burns in me. Every time I take the bread and the cup, I do it in remembrance of Christ, in two ways. First, I picture him, as best I can, on the cross, dying for us all. I try to imagine what it was like for him to bear this world's sins. And the resultant, momentary, separation. The agony of forsakenness. The absence. The disconnect.

As I am writing these words, Linda is away visiting a friend. She is only gone for two days, but I miss her. I miss her with me. Near me. What would it be like, to not have her in my life? I hate the thought! But surely not as much as the thought of the Son being apart from the presence of the Father. As I take communion, I think of such things.

Second, I think of how God rescued me out of my depravity. I hold the little cup in my hand and see lights reflected in the crimson liquid. This, to me, represents the light of Christ descending deep into my darkness,

---

[26] To deepen your theological understanding of the word "in," see Lewis Smedes, *Union with Christ: A Biblical View of the New Life in Christ* (Grand Rapids: Eerdmans, 2009).

[27] Greg Boyd, *Present Perfect*, p. 45. See also John Ortberg, "Experiential Knowledge of the Trinity," in Dallas Willard, *Living in Christ's Presence: Final Words on Heaven and the Kingdom of God*.

pumping the oxygen of life into my lungs, carrying me to the surface. Into his presence. I have been set free, now and forever. *I never forget this.*

Once I was out of his presence, then thrust into his presence.

I have met him.

This is not a religious theory. It is not mere information. It's not a theology. Nor is it a church growth strategy. It is a relationship. With the most important fact of reality.

Dallas Willard writes:

> "The kingdom is available now; I just have to want it more than I want anything else. The Trinity is right here. I don't have to wait. I don't have to be preoccupied. I don't have to have anything solved. In fact, I could say to the world, "Go ahead, bring it on, because nothing can separate me." I just have to want it more than I want anything else. I just have to say, "With God's help in this moment, I will refuse to allow anything to sever that from me.""[28]

In this book I have, hopefully, re-introduced you to God's experienced presence. Like Moses, God's presence-driven people refuse to go or do anything without his presence going with us.

My prayer for you is that you will know God by experience. That you will lead others into his presence. That your church will be living water that satisfies humanity's existential thirst. That you will live the connected life, in Christ.

That you will be driven by his presence. And see God win the day.

---

[28] Dallas Willard, *Living in Christ's Presence*, p. 105.

SUMMING UP – LEADERSHIP POINTS

In summary, I am reasoning as follows.

1. There is a metaphysical impulse in all persons that will not go away.
2. God's presence satisfies this impulse. We find our ultimate fulfillment in him.
3. In presence-driven churches people encounter and experience the God who is the object of their longing and seeking.
4. God's presence wins the day.

Do you agree, or disagree, with these four points?

If you agree with them, how will they affect the shape of your ministry?

Teach and preach these things to your people. I believe they will cause confidence and hope to rise.

Finally, check for updates on my blog (johnpiippo.com), and email me with questions (johnpiippo@msn.com).

Printed in the United States
By Bookmasters